WELCOME TO JAPAN'S DARK SIDE

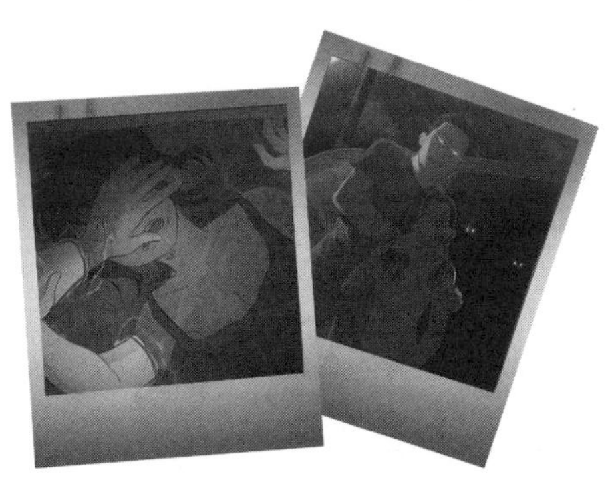

WELCOME TO JAPAN'S DARK SIDE

SENSATIONAL TRUE CRIME CASES THAT WILL SHOCK YOU!

McSkyz

TUTTLE Publishing

Tokyo | Rutland, Vermont | Singapore

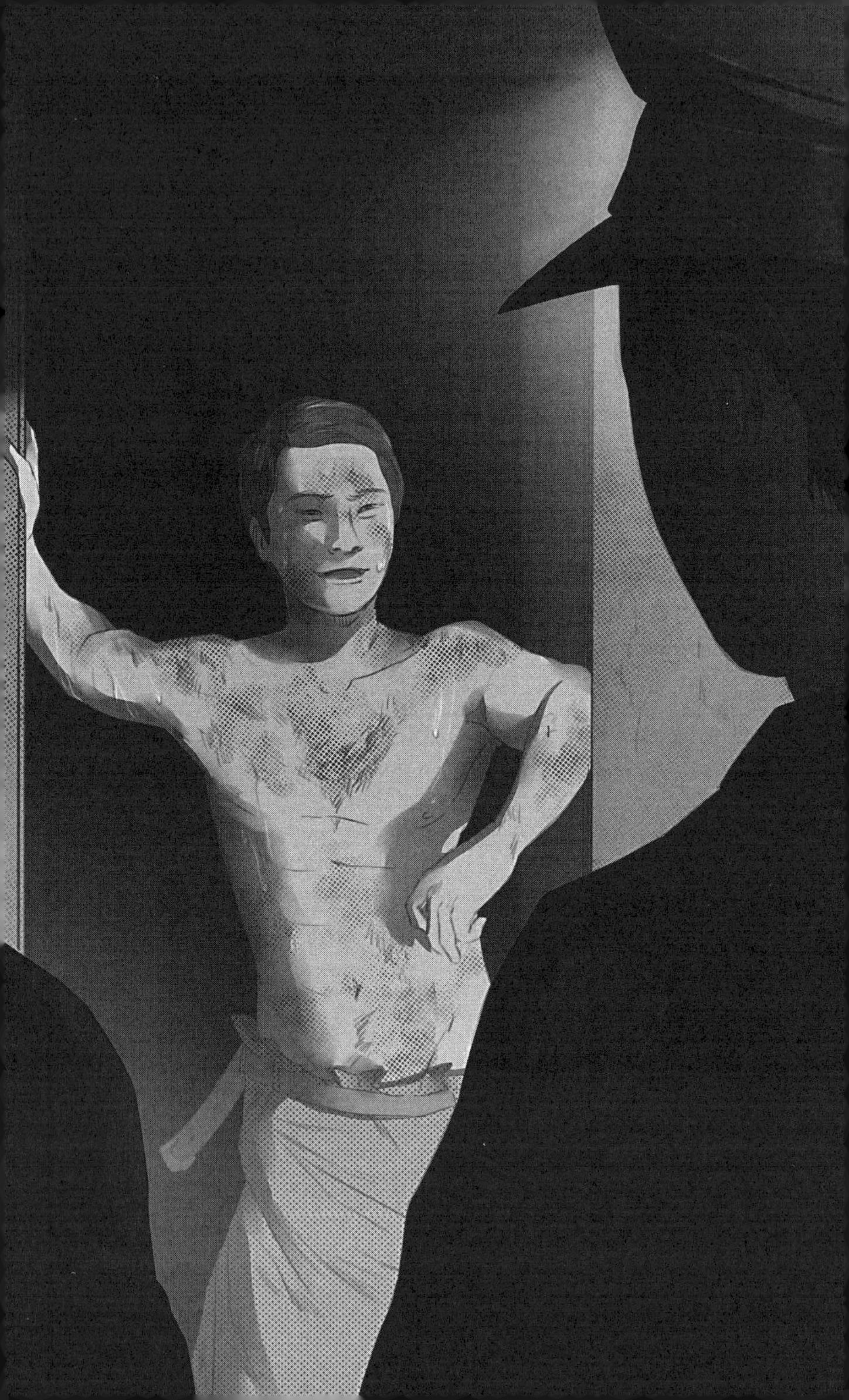

Contents

Welcome to Japan's Dark Side

Most of us—myself included—perceive Japan as a country steeped in tradition, where respect and harmony reign among the populace. Having had the good fortune to visit the country, I can affirm that assertion is true—most of the time.

Behind this smooth facade, there are deviances that, as in every population around the world, reveal a completely different side of the nation.

The pressures to succeed, the societal stress placed on education and career, for example, can lead to desperate deeds. The desire to sidestep failure or the inability to compete or keep up can lead to tragic acts.

The almost blind respect for family authority and reputation, when it compels members to torture or kill, is yet another universal motive and compulsion in the annals of true crime. Entire families, under the sway of Father or Mother's commands, mutilate and dismember even their own relatives.

This volume of eight terrifying tales is set to take you on a journey far beyond the tourist clichés and broad generalizations applied to Japan. So get ready to discover a side of Japan you rarely see, the darkness and shadows that precede the rising sun.

THE MUTOS, A VERY SPECIAL FAMILY

FAMILIES AND THEIR stories... a very complex subject. Relationships between parents, between children, between parents and children, a subject that has fueled our greatest novels, films, plays and television series. . . And then there's the extended family, the supporting players drawn into the web, the cousins, aunts and uncles.... A family tree that grows slowly and surely over time, that's what it's all about. But often, twigs snap off, branches break and are sawn off over time and not necessarily the most rotten limbs. The tree is pruned and trimmed. We try to hide what we don't want others to see.

I've chosen to tell you about the Azumi Muto case, a family affair that has both fascinated and terrorized the whole of Japan. It began in 2007, in Tokyo, among a wealthy family. From the time the story broke, the public became fascinated by the Muto family story, the newspapers and tabloids closely following every twist and turn. Perhaps because their saga puts into perspective many of the setbacks and challenges you may have experienced with your own family.

You're going to need a strong heart to follow my story through to the end, because I have no intention of sparing the rawest details. But if you're a true crime fan already, then you're not expecting the happily-ever-after resolutions of a romance novel.

Marcel Proust wrote: "We get from our family both the ideas we live by and the illness we die of." The Muto story is a perfect illustration of that rather bleak observation. So let me tell you their story. I'm going to take you inside the family fold of a clan like no other—lucky for us!

A HORRIBLE DISCOVERY

On Monday, January 2, 2007, the Muto family returned home to Hatagaya, in Tokyo's Shibuya district. Mamoru, the father, is a 62-year-old dentist, his wife, also a dental practitioner, and Koki is their eldest son. The trio had spent the latter months of 2006 in their home in the Tōhoku region, over 300 miles (483 km) north of Tokyo, a region known for its volcanoes, mountainous landscape and ski slopes. A feast for the eyes, a chance to recharge before returning to the hectic, restless life of Tokyo. An almost therapeutic respite.

The journey home, however, has left them exhausted. They're glad to be back home, where they can meet up with Yuki, their other son, and Azumi, their only daughter, who had other plans to celebrate the new year. Yuki had stayed behind to study for his fourth dental school entrance exam. As for Azumi, the only one in the family who didn't want to continue in the line of caregivers, she was with her theater troupe, rehearsing a play.

The Shibuya district, located southwest of Tokyo's Imperial Palace, reflects the image of this megalopolis, the world's most populous city: wide thoroughfares illuminated day and night by huge flashing billboards, bustling streets. . . . The district is also known as a fashion center. One of its symbols is Tower 109, a shopping mall favored by the capital's affluent young people, as it houses over a hundred boutiques dedicated to the latest fashion trends. Shibuya Station is also one of the busiest in the Tokyo area.

The Mutos push open the door of their apartment and go straight to bed. Yuki has gone off to study at a cram camp with other university students, and Azumi is absent as usual. Theater takes up most of her time. Exhausted, the Mutos soon fall asleep. . . .

The next morning, when the family wakes up, a putrid smell seems to have invaded the whole dwelling. Is it coming from their own home, a neighboring apartment or even the street? Undaunted, the Muto parents rush off to their dental surgery without investigating or asking any questions. Their day is jam-packed with appointments. "I'll take care of that smell when I get back," says the wife.

When the couple return in the evening, the stench is even stronger than in the morning. Mrs. Muto is determined to find the source of the odor: it must be Yuki's or Azumi's fault, as they must have left some food somewhere. Yes, that's got to be it. . . .

It was then that Mamoru remembered what Yuki had told him as they set off for his camp. He had found their dead pet fish in his aquarium.

"Maybe it'll smell a little bad when you get back, but don't worry, I'll take care of everything when I return."

Well, if that's all there is to it then. . . . Yuki's mother rushes off to her son's room, where she discovers the fish in the aquarium . . . but very much alive. That's odd. So if it isn't the fish, what's rotting? The smell is coming from Yuki's room. Yet everything seems to be in order. The bed's made up, everything's in its usual place. But this stench, it's coming from the cupboards? A plate of food has been forgotten on a shelf? Mrs. Muto opens the large cupboard on the right and lets out a terrified scream.

And now their nightmare begins. . . .

THE HAPPY CLAN

The Muto family has always taken care of other people's teeth. They love it, it's their family calling handed down from father to son and from mother to son. Mrs. Muto's parents were dentists, and Mamoru pursued his future wife after she graduated from dental school, to ensure that the family tradition would continue. Her parents were also dentists. In fact, it was Mrs Muto's father who opened a clinic for his daughter and son-in-law, an extension of his own practice established in the 1950s in Hatagaya, a quiet residential area lined with houses and low-rise buildings. So this is a highly respectable family, right? Judge for yourself. . . .

Koki, the eldest son, is studying to become . . . a dentist at Nihon University's dental school, a prestigious private institution. He's in his fifth year and plans to join his parents' practice afterward.

Yuki, the youngest, born in 1985, also aspires to the family trade. He's an intelligent young man, but has recently been diagnosed with a number of mental health problems, including obsessive-compulsive cleanliness disorder, which means that everything around him has to be absolutely clean and tidy. He sometimes washed items or his clothes several times a day. But these compulsions start to get in the way of his studies. His grades suffer. He's a smart kid, but his various behavioral problems aren't helping him on his path through young adulthood.

Although his parents have not said a word about this highly sensitive subject, Yuki has already failed his dental school entrance exam three times. Since graduating from high school, the young man had wanted more than anything to follow in his father's and older brother's footsteps and go to the same school as them. Deep down, after all his failures, Yuki feels ashamed. But he doesn't give up. He studies harder. He knows and feels that his fourth attempt will finally end in success. To make sure he has an escape route, just in case, Yuki studies science along with his cramming. He's very concerned about ecology and the environment. He's obsessed with planting trees and grass; he wants to make the world greener.

He's a good guy and a good friend. But opinions differ on this subject. In his first year of high school, he was vice president of some of his school clubs. Yet he doesn't have many friends. Yuki is described by many—including his classmates and his little sister, Azumi—as a singular, socially awkward young man who takes a long time to integrate himself into a group.

Azumi Muto, the "little one," was born on June 13, 1986. She's kind and compassionate. She takes care of a cat that she adores. She's also the rebel of the family. Scraping plaque deposits off teeth? Putting on crowns and treating the cavities of sugar-addicted children? No way!

Azumi has other plans. One in particular is a driving and increasingly common need in these times: she wants to become famous. To do so, she's chosen the acting profession. She hesitated for a long time over computer science. Why not, if she could have become a Fusajirō Yamauchi, the founder of Nintendo, or the next Steve Jobs. But she chose theater studies instead.

As you can imagine, her parents aren't happy with her career choice and have tried everything to persuade her to follow a more respectable and lucrative path: the daily grind.

But Azumi is determined to escape the Muto family destiny.

In 2004, at the age of 18, she ran away from home for a while. Before leaving home, she left her pet at a cat hotel so that it wouldn't suffer from her absence. For some Japanese child, a runaway child is a source of shame. All the more so as, before running away, Azumi had slashed both her wrists. It was not an actual suicide attempt (although this is still in doubt today), but rather a form of self-mutilation, a warning signal, a cry for help. Azumi may bear the Muto name, but she seemingly did not inherit the family spirit.

She kept in touch with her parents, but wanted above all to be independent, to stand on her own two feet. A friend later testified that Azumi was not a selfish person who sought media attention at all costs, who considered an appearance on a talk show or another appearance in the spotlight as her highest goal. . . . She worked hard for public recognition, but seemed to want above all her family's approval. Her mantra, in autumn 2005, was: "I don't care if I die at any moment." Casual, careless and reckless words of an individual trying to find her place in the world.

Azumi tentatively began an artistic career after working in a boutique as a salesgirl, then as a bar hostess. Her job was to offer companionship to lonely men, without sexual favors. Still very young and inexperienced, Azumi agrees to star in a low-budget erotic film with the evocative name of *Kurîmu remon: Pûru-saido no ami (Lemon Cream: Ami at Poolside)*. On IMDB.com, you'll find this summary:

> *Ami, who grew up in China, is a high-school student who practices Chinese martial arts and swimming. Hiroshi is a carefree student who enjoys secretly photographing women. One day, while practicing his hobby, he and his friend Takomoto enter a girls' changing room at the school swimming pool and run into Ami.*

To keep her family in the dark about her role in the film, she assumed the pseudonym of Kakeru Takamine. Unfortunately for her, Kakeru's career came to a screeching halt. Azumi broke her leg in a bad fall, the accident keeping her away from the set and leaving her with no source of income. Dejected, she is forced to return home to live with her family in 2005.

Once back on her feet, listing with an artists' agency to present her profile to film and television directors, Azumi joins a theater troupe to work on her acting. In December 2005, she makes her first stage appearance in the play "Jumpinger." She never stops talking about her role, telling anyone who will listen that she's finally doing something she enjoys.

She's going out on other auditions and taking the rejections in stride. She's even trying to get in some modeling castings.

It's important to understand that Azumi doesn't hate her parents—far from it—she simply wants to follow a different path from the one they've traced for their three children from an early age. And what better way than to prove to them that she's got what it takes to be an actress than performing in a hit play! The Mutos are slowly warming up to the idea of having an actress daughter. Azumi, the youngest, has always been their favorite, and we need to keep Azumi's free spirit in mind to understand what happens next. For she enrages her brother Yuki, who is totally deferential to his parents. He wants to follow in their footsteps, but because of his emotional and behavioral problems, he can't get his life on track. It's this difference that will fuel the drama to come.

BROTHER AND SISTER: TWO ROOMS, TWO VIBES

Yuki and Azumi have a complex relationship. Yuki spends most of his time studying to pass his dental exams. Azumi, in her own way, also works hard. She takes dubbing lessons, follows online tutorials and goes to numerous castings for acting roles and modeling gigs. Being siblings, a seemingly playful rivalry exists between the two and they constantly tease each other. They also butt heads, bickering and fighting until they stop speaking for a while. But eventually they patch things up. They're brother and sister after all.

For Many Young Japanese, the Pressure Is On!

In some Japanese extended families, starting as early as kindergarten, children are subjected to an enormous amount of academic and societal pressure. They're simply expected to excel. Failure is of course very much frowned upon. Whether it's tying shoelaces independently, mastering cursive handwriting in the first year of school, or getting into the best universities later on, the nation's system focuses on rapid, rigorous and thorough preparation. While in other educational systems, some students are encouraged to repeat a year, for many Japanese students, that's simply not an option. The pupil must advance to the next grade at any cost. For a student who's slipping behind or who can't keep up, the pressure mounts. . . .

When his mental problems aren't getting the better of him, Yuki even helps Azumi out. Especially with her homework. He advises her, guides her, looks after her like a big brother. In fact, Azumi calls Yuki "Isamu." The word is used to denote courage, bravery, success. . . . Was it an ironic choice? Was she making fun of him? We'll never know.

When Yuki falls back into his old ways, it's Azumi and his parents who pay the price. Yuki finds it increasingly difficult to cope with the family pressure. Above all, he finds it hard to accept his sister's actions. Even if she tries to get her parents to support her choices, she's still gone off in her own direction and forged her own nontraditional path.

And that's not all. The Muto's neighbors and visitors have also observed, over time, some very strange behaviors on the part of Yuki toward his sister. There are accounts of the brother's strange, intense glances at her, almost as if he were attracted to her . . . sexually. Some even speculate that Yuki is aware of his sister's participation in "*Lemon Cream*" and has even watched the film several times on the sly. In any case, those who noticed these suggestive signs and behaviors attributed it to either innocent or licentious motives: either he was simply jealous of his socially active sister or he was, indeed, incestuously attracted to her. Ah, families . . . you never know what goes on behind closed doors!

BEFORE THE CLOSET DOOR OPENS

Let's go back to 2007. You'll remember that Mrs. Muto opened the door to her son's closet and let out a scream. So I bet you're eager to know what's inside. Patience . . . I'm only asking for a few pages of patience. . . . First, I'll tell you in detail what happened before that fateful moment.

On December 30, 2006, Mrs. Muto and her eldest son, Kiko, set off for the Tōhoku region to recharge their batteries. The Mutos have relatives in Fukushima, and this getaway also gives them the opportunity to visit them. It was agreed that Mamoru would leave the next day so he could work at the clinic for an additional day. Azumi and Yuki would stay in Tokyo: Azumi to concentrate on her acting and Yuki to attend his cram camp.

Cram Schools in Japan

In Japan, cramming schools—or cram camps—also known as *juku*, are private educational establishments that offer additional instruction to students, usually in preparation for entrance exams to high schools, universities or vocational schools. These schools are very popular in Japan, as the educational system is ultra-competitive and students often feel the need for extra support and preparation to pass their exams on the first try, out of fear of failure. The school program generally focuses on exam preparation, and students can receive tutoring in subjects such as mathematics, science and languages. Yuki has enrolled in a prestigious camp where he is expected to stay until January 11 to prepare for his fourth attempt at the dental entrance exam.

Before she leaves, Mrs. Muto delivers her final instructions to Azumi over the intercom. Dinner is in the fridge, but she's also left some money in case she and Yuki want to order food. She then says goodbye to her daughter before setting off. On December 31, the following day, at around 2 p.m., Mamoru Muto, who has finished his appointments at the clinic, is on his way out. He picks up Yuki at their home (he'd been there all morning with his sister) to take him to his cram camp, then heads off to join his family in the mountains of Fukushima. It's precisely at this moment, when father and son are in the car, that Yuki mentions the death of his pet fish. He promises to get rid of it as soon as possible, as the smell is already pungent. Mamoru doesn't even respond. It's a trifle, a regrettable occurrence in the life of a family pet. He drives north, and the two days of vacation go as well as can be expected.

BEHIND THE CLOSET DOOR

We return to January 2, 2007, at the precise moment when Mrs. Muto opens the closet. She screams. The entire neighborhood could hear her heart-wrenching cry.

She screams, but she doesn't act. Mamoru finds her frozen in place, standing before a heap of trash bags. The nauseating stench of decay is unmistakable. What the two parents are about to discover will shake them to their core—and even beyond that. They can hardly believe it. Inside the bags are body parts: hands, arms, feet. They are holding their breath. What are they truly looking for? The head?

A bag falls from higher up. Mamoru opens it. It is indeed a head—the head of Azumi, their beloved daughter.

Mrs. Muto breaks down. She leaves her son's room screaming, only to collapse in the living room. She weeps, speaking incoherent words and phrases. Mamoru, for his part, feels as though his legs can no longer support him. They feel like cotton. He sits down, burying his head in his hands. The fish story. . . The bags in his son's closet. . . Yuki did this; there is no doubt about it.

The father is not angry. He remains in this state of shock for an hour before finally standing up.

It is now January 3, 2007, at 10:30 p.m. Mamoru enters the Yoyogi police station, part of the Tokyo Metropolitan Police Department.

Before an officer, he recounts the macabre discovery without accusing his beloved son. Mamoru hesitated for a long time but decided it was better to let the police handle the investigation. This time, they should act quickly.

AZUMI

In the report detailing the father's initial statements, he explains that he was alerted by a terrible stench of decay, prompting him and his wife to search the house until they eventually found the bags in their son's closet.

The police arrived immediately on the scene. Mrs. Muto was still in a state of shock. The forensic experts performed their work, taking the bags to the morgue, while the officers noted that there were no signs of forced entry or any evidence of a struggle.

"Mr. Muto," a police officer questioned, "are you sure you're not hiding anything from us?"

Mamoru broke down. He mentioned the dead fish, implicating Yuki. How could he have done otherwise?

On the morning of January 4, Yuki Muto was arrested at his cram school for the murder of his sister. Among his belongings, investigators found a pair of panties belonging to Azumi. Yuki allowed himself to be arrested without any resistance. More than that: he immediately confessed to the murder and agreed to fully cooperate with the authorities. He promised to tell everything.

BACKSTAGE ACTION

You are about to read the exhaustive and highly detailed account of Azumi's murder, a crime committed by her own brother, Yuki. This reconstruction of the hours leading up to the act was made possible thanks to Yuki's testimony, of course, as well as the work of the police and their forensic technicians.

Brace yourselves.

It's December 30, 2006, 3 p.m. Azumi is watching television. Yuki walks in and sits next to his sister. He wants to relax in front of a show too, but Azumi starts pestering him:

"Don't you have exams to prepare for?" she says.

Yuki doesn't just shrug it off. He gets annoyed. Why doesn't she mind her own business? Can he never get a moment's peace? He snaps at his sister, the argument escalates, tempers flare, and insults are exchanged. "Anyway," the young woman says, "you don't even have a dream! I do! And I'm working hard to make it a reality one day."

Yuki is shaken by his sister's words, which he believes to be untrue. He does have a dream: to take over their parents' dental practice with his brother. Is that dream somehow worth less than Azumi's ambitions of fame?

He starts yelling at his sister, who immediately bursts into tears at the harshness of his words. At that moment, Yuki holds himself back from getting physical. Azumi jumps off the futon and heads to the bathroom to wash her face. Yuki takes the opportunity to go back to his room—it's better that way.

But in his room, the young man continues to brood over his anger. He can't take it anymore. He feels his brain heating up; he can't calm down. Who is she to lecture him like that? Will he never be the model son everyone expects him to be? Why did he have to be burdened with these obsessive-compulsive tendencies?

Yuki's eyes land on a kendo sword hanging on the wall. It's made entirely of bamboo, resembling the traditional katana, whose blade is made of steel. Samurai used such swords to practice the art of kendo. With these weapons, you strike rather than cut. But in the hands of someone skilled, it can be a devastating weapon, capable of targeting an opponent's vulnerable points.

Yuki takes the sword off the wall and looks for Azumi. She is in the bathroom on the second floor, which is rarely used. She is wiping away the makeup that has smeared because of her tears.

Yuki strikes her for the first time from behind, hitting her on the head. He has lost control of himself. He strikes, and strikes again. Azumi screams, tries to flee, and defends herself. She turns to her brother, trying to reason with him, but Yuki is no longer listening—he hears only his anger. He hits his sister in the face, several times; her face quickly becomes swollen and bruised.

This series of blows of unprecedented violence broke Azumi's will to defend herself. She crawls, curling up in a corner of the bathroom, and starts complaining about the cold. She is very cold, she is frozen. Yuki has no intention of warming her up, quite the opposite. He grabs a towel lying on the floor and wraps it around

Azumi's neck. He tightens it tightly. As tightly as possible. The young woman is too weak to defend herself. It's this moment that the murderer recalls a true crime TV show he had seen not long ago, where he had learned that it took one hundred and eighty seconds to strangle someone to death... Azumi tries to speak, but Yuki tightens even harder. Three minutes is a long time. When he finally lets go of the towel, he leans toward his sister's mouth and sees that she is still breathing. His anger intensifies, if that is even possible. Yuki drags her to the bathtub, drops her in, and turns on the water taps. Once the tub is a third full, he holds his sister's head under the water. Exhausted, Azumi can no longer defend herself, nor raise herself up. She gives up. This time, Yuki has succeeded. Not on the first try. But on the third. His anger decreases as the minutes pass.

The calm has returned to the house. His sister's body floats in the reddened water of the bathtub. Through the window, a faint light allows him to still distinguish day from night. Yuki then realizes the chaos in the bathroom. There is blood everywhere. He has it on him too, on his face, his mouth, his nostrils—his sister scratched him fiercely. Should he clean all of this up now? No. He has better things to do. He absolutely must dispose of this body, hide his crime... He can think clearly again. And he does.

Yuki goes downstairs to the kitchen and spots a large, very sharp knife, the one his mother uses to cut herbs when preparing the family's ramen. In the garage, he grabs a saw. Then he goes back upstairs to the bathroom and cuts his sister's body into fifteen pieces. This takes more than one hundred and eighty seconds...

He saws through the joints of the legs, arms, abdomen, and head. Then he disperses the body into four double-thick plastic garbage bags (one can never be too careful).

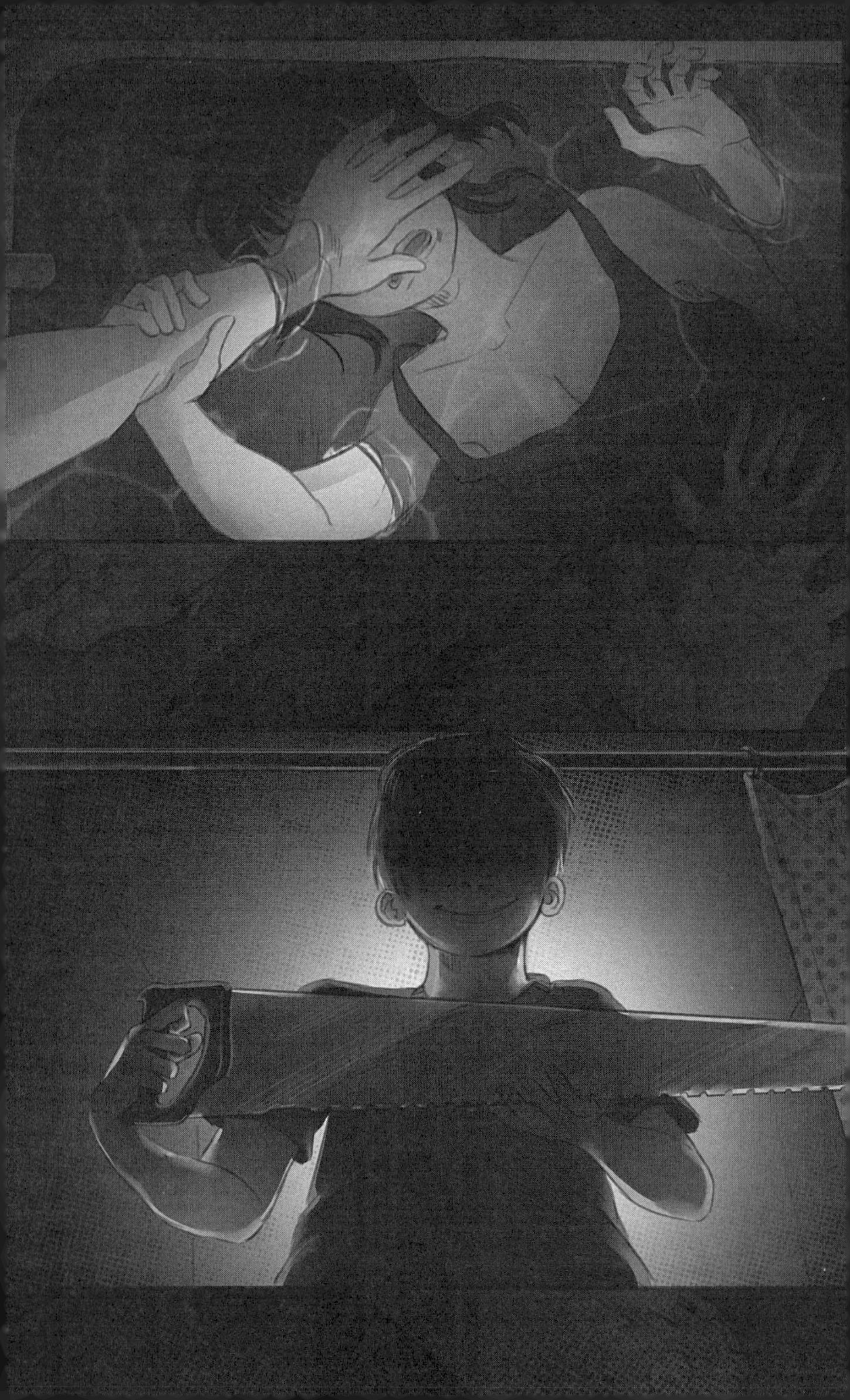

He throws his sister's lower abdomen and breasts into the bathroom trash. Why? Because at this moment, he thinks it will hinder the process of identifying the body. If neither the vagina nor the breasts of the victim are found, then they won't be able to tell whether it's a man or a woman. Then Yuki hides three bags in the closet of his room, which is on the third floor of the house, and one in his wardrobe.

Then, he meticulously cleans the bathroom, so thoroughly that, later, when the forensic technicians comb through the house to confirm Yuki's testimony, they won't find a single bloodstain in the room, even with the famous Luminol, which reveals them for sure, even many years later. The only trace of blood will be found in the bathtub drain, as well as on the walls of the second-floor hallway; likely blood cast off by Yuki when he went downstairs to retrieve the knife and the saw.

Of course, as soon as this dreadful news is made public, the press gathers outside the home of this wealthy and famous couple of dentists. A crime like this in a family of prominent citizens? Television trucks and dozens of journalists flood the quiet street of Hatagaya.

This, however, doesn't stop the investigators from continuing their search. And it's the autopsy that reveals very troubling details about Azumi's death. Yuki hasn't really told everything...

Sure, there were signs of strangulation on the neck, head injuries caused by a blunt object, and water in the victim's lungs.

But... according to the medical examiners, the method of dismemberment resembled that of a specialist, someone experienced in this kind of act, and it required specialized medical knowledge. For example, the knife was inserted each time into areas of the body that were easy to penetrate and then provided easier access to the joints.

Did Yuki know these techniques? Had he learned them from the numerous true crime documentaries he watched on TV? This raised some suspicions... Could the young Japanese man have had an accomplice?

A Similar Case in the Shibuya Area

An interesting note for true crime enthusiasts like yourselves. . . Around the same time, a somewhat similar case unfolded in the same Shibuya district, just a few miles from the Muto residence.

The body of Yusuke Mitsuhashi was discovered, also dismembered. This dismemberment murder case began with the discovery of the upper half of a body in Shinjuku (a nearby district) and the lower half in Shibuya.

The part of the body found in Shinjuku was the upper torso, missing the head, arms, and lower body. It was completely naked, with the left hand severed at the elbow, the right wrist missing, and the lower body cut about 2 inches (5 cm) below the navel. The lower half of the body was found face down in the garden of an empty private house in Shibuya, with a flowerpot placed inside it. The head was discovered in Serigaya Park, in the city of Machida.

The proximity of the two crimes and the similar dismemberment methods initially led investigators to suspect a connection to the Azumi Muto case.

Yusuke, the victim, was known to frequent hostess bars, particularly establishments where Azumi had worked during her time on the run. Investigators hypothesized that Azumi might have become Yusuke's mistress.

The Tokyo police carried out an intensive investigation, which led to the arrest of Yusuke Mitsuhashi's wife, Kaori Mitsuhashi.

Kaori admitted to dismembering her husband's body in the living room of their apartment in Tomigaya, in the Shibuya district. However, no traces of blood were found in the area where the dismemberment allegedly took place. Renovation work had been done in the apartment, raising suspicions.

Similar actions had been undertaken. Yet another similarity with Azumi's murder and the absence of blood traces in the bathroom. That being said, the wife would have worked with accomplices. In the end, only Kaori Mitsuhashi was convicted in this case. She received fifteen years in prison. She did, in fact, benefit from mitigating circumstances, as it was established during the trial that her husband had frequently subjected her to domestic violence. From this perspective, we are indeed straying from our case. . .

Other terrible elements: it's known that Yuki cut off his sister's breasts and removed her vagina so that the sex of the corpse could not be determined. But the medical examiners reported that Azumi's body had also been meticulously washed before being dismembered, and that Yuki had shaved the pubic hair, as well as all other body hair, with great care. He also removed all the internal organs from the chest (heart, lungs, etc.) to gather them in a bag.

During his interrogation, Yuki remained as calm as can be. He told the investigators all of this without emotion, as if recounting a fictional story. After dismembering his sister's body, he told the investigators that he made himself a generous pork sandwich and then, once the bags were closed and placed in the closets, he treated himself to a good nap during which he claimed to have slept "deeply." Upon waking, a thought occurred to him: now, Azumi would no longer provoke him about his lack of success, and he could truly focus on his studies. Between the lines, it can be read that her murder had a therapeutic effect on him.

During this phase of the investigation, the dozens of journalists gathered outside the Muto residence questioned neighbors, classmates of the victim and the murderer, as well as family members. Many rumors were then spread... It was said that Yuki had taken his nap after the murder with his sister's head on the pillow, or that he had had a post-mortem sexual relationship with her. A friend of Azumi stated that the young woman had confided in him that she had been sexually harassed by her brother. Neighbors also contributed to the rumors, telling stories about Mamoru, Azumi's father, regularly hitting his daughter. To this, Mamoru directly responded: "I hit her as part of her education, but it wasn't serious. I was never violent enough to cause her injuries. The last time was when she was in her first year of high school." As a defense, could it get any worse?

The rumors are flying, the press is buzzing around Azumi's murder, and the shockwave is enormous in Japan. But Mamoru has developed a taste for speaking out. Since he's being asked to speak, he will do so. At length. This is the continuation of this very peculiar case. . .

MAMORU MUTO'S STATEMENTS

Did he do this because he felt harassed by the press or to free his conscience? We have chosen to reproduce here, in full, the statements made by Azumi's father:

"I would like to take this opportunity to sincerely apologize for causing a great deal of concern and worry to the entire country due to the incident involving my son Yuki. To be honest, my family and I are in a state of mind where we can't even recall exactly what happened since New Year's, when we first learned about the incident.

Our family is deeply troubled by the fact that we cannot connect the death of our daughter, Azumi, to the violent actions of our second son. Even my family is in this situation, so I know it's even harder for the general public to understand.

About twenty days have passed since the events, and as the police investigation progresses, the facts are gradually coming to light, but I still don't understand why my son committed such a violent act. However, over time, I've been able to think more calmly, and my mind is clearer now than it was a few days ago.

First, regarding the relationship between Azumi and Yuki, it was reported that they had a cold relationship and hadn't spoken for over three years, but the truth is different. However, it is true that Azumi's free-spirited personality and behavior, which disregarded others, were not understood by her family. Yuki, who is only a year older than Azumi, came to believe that his younger sister was a source of problems for us, her parents.

As for Yuki's personality, I can assure you that he is a kind young man and has never exhibited any violent behavior toward his family. Unfortunately, his younger sister, Azumi, thrived on conflict, and she was a child who could never admit her mistakes or apologize.

However, both of our children are irreplaceable to us. Now, in hindsight, I wonder why Azumi didn't apologize to her brother after provoking him on the day of the murder. If she had apologized, I am sure Yuki would have regained his composure and wouldn't have committed such atrocious acts.

My wife and I will continue to mourn the spirit of Azumi for the rest of our lives, and we will continue to support Yuki so that he can recover as quickly as possible.

We ask that you kindly give us some time until we are able to regain a little peace of mind."

The victim's father's statement will strongly anger Azumi's friends. Many testify, claiming that the father is desperately trying to defend his son and that the little love he had for his daughter is evident in his final statements. It always comes back to this story of the ugly duckling. . . Azumi refused to become a dentist. Could the father have thought that she ultimately paid the price for it?

YUKI'S JUDGMENT

On February 9, 2007, the Tokyo Metropolitan Police announced that four important pieces of evidence had been lost. When Yuki was arrested on January 4, investigators had placed sports shoes, a sweatshirt, the saw, and a kendo sword in a cardboard box, which an investigator from the first division mistook for trash and subsequently discarded. That's quite a mess, isn't it?

Despite the loss of these critical crime tools (to put it mildly), the remaining evidence was sufficient to charge Yuki with the murder of his sister, as well as the serious charge of corpse desecration.

On May 12, 2008, less than a year and a half after the crime, the Tokyo District Court found Yuki Muto guilty of murder but acquitted him of the mutilation and dismemberment of the body. Why? Yuki was found to be mentally impaired. His psychological state, including obsessive-compulsive disorder and several other conditions, led to a reduced sentence. He received seven years in prison.

However, on April 28, 2009, the Tokyo High Court overturned the previous judgment and sentenced him to twelve years in prison. After a final appeal, on September 16 of the same year, the Supreme Court confirmed the second-instance verdict.

Yuki therefore served twelve years in prison for his atrocities.

As you may have guessed from the dates mentioned. . . Yuki Muto is free as of now. You could very well encounter him on the streets during your future stay in Tokyo. He was released from prison in 2021 and returned to live with his. . . family. Surrounded by the love of his father, mother, and older brother.

Often, in families, there are those who are considered the ugly ducklings. Yes. But they aren't necessarily the ones who deserve it. . .

FUTOSHI MATSUNAGA, A PERVERT'S PROXY MURDERS

THE TIME HAS come to introduce the story of Futoshi Matsunaga, a deeply disturbing figure in Japanese criminal history. The typical image of a serial killer, something heavily influenced by cinema, often conjures up a grotesque, isolated figure in a filthy home. However, Futoshi Matsunaga challenges this stereotype in a chilling way. He was not a hands-on killer, but rather a manipulator who orchestrated horrific murders without directly committing the acts himself. His story is even more unsettling because of the psychological control he exerted over his followers, using them as instruments to carry out his grotesque crimes.

The narrative seems to dive deep into the psychological complexities of manipulation, power, and the disturbing notion of "murder by proxy." It raises the question of how someone can orchestrate a series of killings without getting their hands dirty, and the chilling effect of the power they wield over others. This twist adds an extra layer of horror to the case, as it forces readers to confront the unsettling reality that a person's control and influence over others can lead to devastating consequences, without them ever directly participating in the violence.

If you'd like a further breakdown or more details on Matsunaga's story, feel free to ask.

Our disclaimer: in this story, the first names of the female victims have all been invented. They were, in fact, never made public.

THE ORIGINS OF EVIL

Let's begin by discussing the young Futoshi Matsunaga. The development of a serial killer's mind is said to begin in childhood, and all psychiatrists agree on this. One must delve into the early years of their life to try to understand their downward spiral. One doesn't become a serial killer by simply waking up one day; it is a slow development of the psyche, shaped by a multitude of acts and episodes experienced in childhood.

Futoshi Matsunaga was born on April 28, 1961, on the island of Kyūshū in Japan. It is the southernmost of Japan's four main islands and the third largest by size. It is surrounded by the waters of the East China Sea to the west, the Philippine Sea to the southeast, the Seto Inland Sea to the northeast, and the Sea of Japan to the north. A true maritime crossroads, Kyūshū was where rice was introduced to Japan from the Korean Peninsula thousands of years ago, a key ingredient in Japanese cuisine. Kyūshū is considered the birthplace of Japanese civilization. Nagasaki, located to the northwest of the island, became infamous for being the site of the second atomic bomb dropped by the United States during World War II in 1945.

Matsunaga lived about 60 miles (100 km) from Nagasaki, in Yanagawa, a former feudal city often referred to as the "Little Venice of Kyūshū." The city is crisscrossed with numerous canals that give it a unique charm. Hayao Miyazaki, the creator of the famous Studio Ghibli, even fell in love with the village during one of his visits. He commissioned a documentary about the city, which helped make Yanagawa a popular destination for both Japanese and international tourists.

It was in this idyllic atmosphere, surrounded by canals, beautifully decorated boats gliding along calm waters, and majestic willows, that Futoshi grew up. His father ran a tatami shop, selling the traditional straw mats covered with rush used to cover Japanese floors. Thanks to the success of the family business, they lived quite comfortably. The young boy lacked for nothing. His mother and grandmother doted on him and spoiled him whenever they could.

Futoshi excels in school. His teachers describe him as an intelligent child. It's not uncommon for him to bring home report cards with nothing but "5" marks, the highest grade in Japan ("1" being the worst, you're welcome for the clarification!). He is charismatic, able to make friends with both boys and girls. Popular, despite his tendency to express strong opinions on a variety of topics, he is quickly elected class president. He joins the student council and is selected as captain of the volleyball team. One of the defining traits of his personality is his desire to be a leader, even if he doesn't necessarily take on his roles with the quality one would expect. For example, during matches, he doesn't really encourage his team or try to unite the players, instead letting his own ego take center stage.

So, is this innate sense of camaraderie, this charming personality, just a facade? Yes, because it soon starts to crack. The skilled and gifted speaker is also, and most notably, a liar. He doesn't hesitate to invent or distort facts, such as his supposed success in a famous speech contest that no one has ever been able to find any record of.

Over time, Futoshi gets in trouble with teachers, particularly due to his disobedience to school rules. He answers back sharply to his teachers, disrupts the class with outbursts and remarks. At first, people think it's just the result of his excess energy and powerful mind always on the loose. But they're wrong, of course. The future will prove that something much darker is developing inside him. He will soon sow not chaos. . . but death.

But what do parents say about this dismissal? Specialists will explain to you that the influence of the family is decisive in understanding the actions of a serial killer.

Well, in truth, not much. Since his birth, Futoshi was destined to take over the tatami business, end of story. So, there was no need to waste too much time and money on university; it was better to get the son into the workforce quickly, give him a job in the family business, and set him on the right track in life.

A job—once his secondary school studies were completed, he took over the shop—and a wife. In 1980, at the age of 19, his parents arranged for him to marry a loving woman. The young couple quickly had a son. Despite his young age, Futoshi already had a well-established life. He left the tatami business to sell futons, the traditional Japanese bedding. His family presented an image of happiness and prosperity. But, once again, it's essential not to shy away from lifting the veil, because Futoshi, an incorrigible flirt, collected mistresses. . . He is said to have had around ten, including Junko Ogata.

JUNK

His affair with her was the real gateway to the unspeakable. What unfolded during their affair lies on the threshold of everything that would happen afterward. If something had been noticed at that moment, if someone close to Futoshi had raised the alarm, if Junko Ogata herself had fought back, then most likely, everything else could have been avoided.

JUNKO OGATA, THE PUPPET

In 1982, Futoshi Matsunaga, 21 years old, is bored in his marriage. He doesn't have a paternal instinct and knows he's not good at the whole monogomy thing. One day, he's flipping through his graduation yearbook and comes across Junko's photo. It's love at first sight, and he doesn't hesitate to contact her. At the time, Junko is a kindergarten teacher in Kurume. Junko knows very little about Futoshi. They barely spoke in high school, but she remembers a rather charming boy who caught the attention of other girls and showed off at school events. It doesn't hurt to have a drink with him, right?

Well, yes, Junko... Yes... And that first meeting? You'll pay dearly for it, unfortunately for you...

Of course, Futoshi is careful not to mention his family situation and lets the young woman talk instead. Junko was born in Kurume, where she teaches, into a wealthy and well-known family. Her father was the director of the local agricultural cooperative association, a notable figure. Junko is charming, gentle, and hardworking. She loves children and has just graduated as a teacher.

In October 1982, while they meet again, Futoshi tells Junko that he wants to marry a great girl. Junko smiles politely. The connection is good, even though Junko is not particularly attracted to the futon salesman. This is when the first incident happens, the first act of violence. As he drives Junko home, Futoshi suddenly stops the car in a dark corner and tries to kiss her, but she resists. It's a clear "no." Futoshi gets the message. In a world governed by logic, Junko should have ended all contact with him, obviously. But the human mind is rarely rational. Other factors come into play. Which ones? No one really knows. Why does the teacher agree to see Futoshi again and again, even after he reveals that he is married and has children, starting a twisted relationship that will inevitably drag her into the abyss?

Through their encounters, Futoshi, judging Junko mature enough to handle it, pushes the boundaries of perversion further and invites her to his home. There, Futoshi wastes no time revealing his true nature. He assaults Junko and abuses, both mentally and physically, his wife, who, unfortunately, is accustomed to such treatment. The man no longer has just one victim at his mercy but two.

One evening, he forces Junko to lick mayonnaise that he has spread in thick trails across the floor, in the presence of his wife and their very young son. The wife steps in to defend a Junko who is more submissive than ever. She is used to fighting back; Junko will marshal such spirit or strength. The descent into hell continues for the teacher. Once so radiant and positive, she is slipping and sinking.

Another harrowing episode: the day Futoshi learns that Junko had an affair before meeting him, he flies into a rage and demands to read his victim's diary. Overwhelmed, Junko asks what she can do to regain his trust, to ease his pain. In a completely matter-of-fact tone, the man declares: "You must tattoo my name on one of your thighs and also carve it into your chest, engraving each letter with a burning cigarette."

Once again, let us question the role of the parents. . . Didn't Junko's deteriorating state and her numerous injuries alarm her family? Of course, they did. They did everything in their power to put an end to this toxic relationship, especially since it was with a married man—Junko had confided this to her aunt—which was utterly unacceptable to them. But how could they completely and decisively destroy this disgraceful affair? Shizumi, Junko's mother, pleaded with her daughter, urging her to end it by any means necessary. Were her arguments starting to resonate?

Futoshi had no intention of backing down. He was the manipulator, after all. And once again, Matsunaga used this family intervention to tighten his grip on the helpless teacher.

He called Shizumi and arranged a meeting at a love hotel in the suburbs of Kurume. There, he tried to seduce her, taking his depravity to the point of initiating physical contact with his victim's own mother. Futoshi then went to Junko and, feigning shock, claimed that Shizumi had tried to seduce him and that he had even had to refuse to engage in a sexual relationship with her.

Hours later, Shizumi's version of events held little weight when she explained it to her daughter. Junko was deeply under the manipulator's influence, and this incident only served to secure her further, both physically and mentally, in his clutches.

Over the months, the teacher weakens at an alarming rate. In February 1985, she collapses in the middle of class, in front of her students, a victim of her crippling anxiety and a staggering lack of sleep. A few days later, on February 13 to be precise, Junko attempts suicide at her parents' home. But once again, Futoshi turns the situation to his advantage, convincing her that her miserable condition is entirely due to the toxic relationship she has with her parents and family—people who, he claims, feel visceral shame toward her and are on the verge of cutting all ties.

Junko believes him and agrees to move in with him, into his family home, alongside his legal wife and son. She resigns from her kindergarten teaching position. From that moment on, she becomes a prisoner.

Fueled by the toxic relationship he has maintained for over three long years, the darkness in Matsunaga's mind grows, like a tumor destined to spread and completely consume him. Just look at what happens next. . .

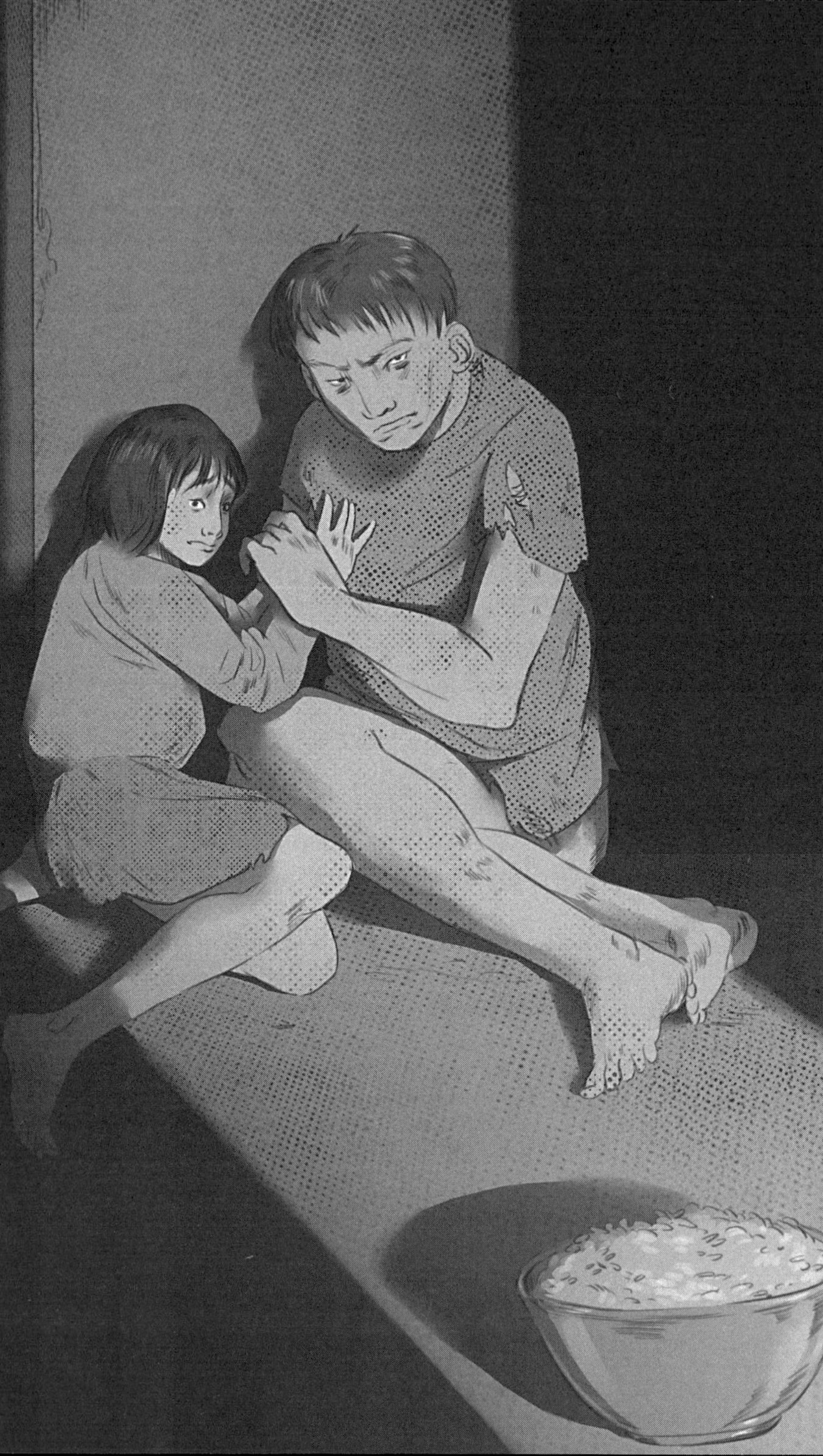

THE FIRST VICTIMS

Outwardly, the establishes his reputation and makes his way in society. In 1985, he builds a three-story steel-framed building near his parents' home. This becomes the headquarters of his company, World, which sells futons. . . worldwide. From here, he oversees his seemingly respectable and thriving business with the help of six employees. In the neighborhood, he is well-liked. . . though far beyond what he deserves.

Inwardly, he is the Master. He takes far more than he gives. He holds human minds under his control, and these are no longer just high school girls or friends subjected to his attentions.

Now, he possesses two women—his wife and his girlfriend—as well as his son. But he doesn't stop there; he turns his attention to his employees as well.

These workers live in a wooden structure located in the courtyard of the business, consisting of a single communal living space. Each evening, he locks the door and windows. For dinner, he rations out the leftovers from his own meals and those of his managers—barely enough to sustain an adult. Creeping behind them, he waves a black rosary he pulls from the pocket of his luxurious double-breasted suit, shouting to terrify them: "*There is a spirit behind you! It's draining your fortune!*" He speaks of *samsara* (the cycle of reincarnation) and *kaimyo* (a Japanese term for a departed soul). Some believed he was even possessed, but that wasn't the case—he subscribed to no religion.

He also forces his employees to lie and engage in illegal business practices. They deceive clients by selling low-quality futons at exorbitant prices, falsely advertising them as "health mattresses." To those who resisted, he would whisper a single word into their ear: "*Yakuza*"—a chilling reference to the local mafia, implying that anyone who left the company, along with their entire family, wouldn't live long. He used the same tactic on customers as well.

How could they all accept this? Control.

A terrible, irresistible force. A phenomenon that unfolds in three stages: appropriation, domination, and imprinting—both physical and psychological marks. Control is established over time, as the aggressor targets fragile minds, exploiting their vulnerabilities. It's a form of brainwashing: intimidation, threats, and absolute control over even the smallest details. The victims are also isolated from their family, friends, social life, and work, cutting off any potential allies if they might consider escaping.

Proud of himself and more satisfied than ever, Futoshi Matsunaga decided it was time to move on to something more extreme. He began preparing to kill.

This was the next step—the logical progression in his twisted mind. Perhaps he even saw it as justified.

To escalate his cruelty, he constructed a soundproofed room on the third floor of his company headquarters, ominously called the Electricity Room. Each time Futoshi was dissatisfied with an employee's performance—or sometimes for no reason at all—he summoned his future victim to this room. There, two of his subordinates would bind the victim's hands and ankles with metal wires and connect them to an electrical outlet.

One victim later gave a harrowing testimony:

"It felt like my brain was being struck with an iron bar. I lost consciousness for a while, but I always woke up with a burning pain in my hands and feet. Even after the electrocution was over, the electricity seemed to linger in my body. Whenever I grabbed the door handle, it would fly open violently."

An employee would later describe every day under Matsunaga as "hell." The word sounds weak to my ears, and I hope it does to yours as well.

It's worth noting that Futoshi himself rarely carried out the torture. He gave the orders, delegating the task to his subordinates or accomplices. Sometimes, he even forced Junko to participate. While the torment unfolded, Futoshi would lie on a futon, casually texting future conquests.

In 1992, Matsunaga's legal wife finally reached her breaking point. Unable to endure any more, she fled and filed for divorce. She had occasionally resisted her husband—perhaps for the sake of their son—but she was not deeply enough under his control to remain. Matsunaga let her go, as she was no longer useful to him. The broken-spirited Junko became his main focus.

Junko remains loyal—devoted to the point of complicity. She aids him in every way. Together, they form the new couple, managing to embezzle and illegally transfer an astonishing 180 million yen ($1.25 million) from the company's accounts into Matsunaga's personal account over seven years.

Of course, such a massive fraud doesn't go unnoticed. Financial authorities begin scrutinizing World closely—very closely. The company, bled dry, racks up over 90 million yen in debt ($600,000), and as word spreads, the remaining employees finally leave.

Futoshi's aura of control and his iron grip on others begin to wane. Left with no options, he chooses the only path available to him: escape. Junko and Futoshi abandon their apartment and head to Ishikawa Prefecture, located 550 miles (900 km) north of Yanagawa, in the central-northern region of Honshu, Japan's largest island. Disappearing under false names, they attempt to evade the authorities now hot on their trail.

An ordinary person might have surrendered or gone into hiding, avoiding any further attention. Matsunaga, however, did the exact opposite. Confident in his self-proclaimed greatness, he decided to escalate his illegal activities.

Once the stolen funds were completely spent, the fugitive had to act. Accustomed to a lavish lifestyle, he needed to come up with a new source of income—and quickly. But his twisted mind wasted no time finding a way to make money without effort, as legitimate work was entirely out of the question.

First, Futoshi had no intention of dirtying his hands. Second, his forged documents limited where he could present himself. Always calculating, Matsunaga operated with one goal in mind: maximizing his benefit. Financially. Sexually. But most of all, in a way that fed his perverse desires.

He began meeting women. To charm them, he introduced Junko as his sister and their newborn son, born in 1993, as his nephew. This familial façade softened his targets, women seeking a stable relationship with a seemingly kind man. His smooth-talking manner sealed the deal, with promises of marriage dangling as bait.

One such encounter led him to a married woman with three children. Deeply charmed and expertly manipulated, she fell in love with Futoshi, eventually abandoning her husband. Playing the devoted partner, he persuaded her to demand money from her ex-husband and her parents. Swayed by his promises of marriage, she handed over 11.8 million yen in cash ($80,000).

But Futoshi wasn't satisfied. He knew he could extract even more—and he intended to.

October 29, 1993. A manipulated woman takes her youngest child, just one year old, to the hospital, accompanied by Junko. "Doctor, it's terrible. . . My child fell off a chair and hit her head," she explains. The doctor conducts the usual examinations, his concerned expression revealing the gravity of the situation. "This baby is suffering from an acute subdural hematoma inside the skull. Its life is in danger," he says gravely.

The diagnosis is barely delivered before the child succumbs to the injuries, right before the eyes of their mother—and Junko.

A tragic domestic accident. That is the conclusion of the medical and judicial authorities. Why not? But could this have been the work of Matsunaga? Was this the first time he caused blood to be spilled without dirtying his own hands? The truth remains elusive.

Five months later, on March 31, 1994, the devastated mother takes her own life, jumping from a bridge into Beppu Bay.

To Matsunaga, her suicide registers merely as a net loss. He treats it with the same detached indifference as if crossing off a client from the old ledgers of World, reducing her to nothing more than a source of profit now extinguished.

It was time to find a new target. Futoshi began his search. Seducing women had worked for a while, but now he wanted someone vile and devious, like himself—someone he could manipulate and control with certainty. A rigged cockfight where the victor would undoubtedly be named Futoshi.

He didn't have to dig deep into his memories to find such a person. He remembered Kumio Toraya, a real estate agent from

Yanagawa, the town of his childhood—and his former success. Back in the glory days of World, the two had been drinking buddies, spending countless nights intoxicated on whiskey, gin and sake. During one of those drunken evenings, Kumio had let slip a dark truth: he had a criminal past and owed a large sum of money to dangerous people—the yakuza. The gangs. The mafia.

At the time, Futoshi had merely nodded, taking note like the master manipulator he was. Now, he saw an opportunity to exploit the desperate man's secrets.

Kumio now lived in Kitakyūshū, a city at the northernmost tip of Futoshi's home island. One morning, Matsunaga and Junko arrived unannounced at the real estate agent's home, where he lived with his 10-year-old daughter, Ren, an adorable little girl.

Futoshi wasted no time in laying out the terms:

"Either we move in with you, or I reveal your secret to the wrong people."

Trapped with no way out, Kumio relented.

Thus began a harrowing nightmare for both him and his daughter Ren—a nightmare that would play out over two years.

Matsunaga and his companion kept Kumio and his daughter, Ren, captive in their own apartment, reducing their existence to a living hell. They forced Kumio to beg for money from his relatives to sustain their lavish lifestyle. Meanwhile, the abuse began—gradually escalating as the captivity dragged on.

Father and daughter were given only meager scraps of food—small portions of rice or leftovers from ramen bowls. Futoshi would time their meals, and if they failed to finish within the allotted time, he would withhold their next portion. They were allowed to use the bathroom no more than once a day, forcing them to relieve themselves into plastic bottles.

Day by day, Kumio and Ren were stripped of any sense of ownership over their home. Matsunaga and Junko confined the pair to a small area, marked off with cardboard boxes, where they were permitted to sleep. The rest of the apartment became the domain of their captors. Over time, they were forced to sleep in a large wooden box, locked from the outside, until Matsunaga decided even that was too comfortable. From then on, their nights were spent on the cold bathroom floor, cushioned only by a few magazines, with their sleep limited to just four hours a night.

As if malnourishment and sleep deprivation weren't enough, Futoshi escalated his cruelty. He instructed Junko to administer electric shocks to Kumio. The real estate agent, now utterly broken, was made to eat his meals directly off the floor and was even forced to consume his own feces. During these sessions, Matsunaga laughed gleefully, photographing the suffering for his own twisted amusement.

Kumio's body bore the terrible evidence of the relentless torture. Constant electric shocks left his skin covered in scabs, while his arms and legs swelled so severely that he could no longer move them. Meanwhile, Ren was subjected to her own torment. Upon returning from school, she was forced to stand for hours in the bathroom without rest. Her academic performance plummeted, yet her teacher failed to intervene or even raise questions.

The depravity of their captors consumed every facet of Kumio and Ren's lives, reducing them to mere shadows of their former selves, while Matsunaga reveled in their despair.

The horror reached its peak when Matsunaga forced Ren to participate in the torture, compelling her to bite her own father. As with all nightmares, this one eventually came to an end, though it was far from merciful. After two grueling years of unimaginable suffering, Kumio's body finally gave out. On February 26, 1996, the real estate agent died of heart failure at the age of 34—a time meant for living, not for dying. Matsunaga, ever the manipulative monster, convinced Ren that her father's death was her fault. He even made her write a letter blaming herself for his demise, a document he kept as a twisted insurance policy for his crimes. What followed defied the bounds of human decency. Matsunaga, having crossed every imaginable line, ordered Ren to assist in dismembering her father's body. Junko then used a blender to grind the body parts, disposing of the remains in the sea near the Kunisaki Peninsula, at the eastern edge of the island. After Kumio's death, Ren remained with Matsunaga, Junko and their child. They adopted a new identity, calling themselves the Hashimoto family. The fact that Ren stayed with her father's murderers speaks to the total psychological control Matsunaga was able to exert over those who fell under his influence. His ability to break and dominate even the most vulnerable minds created a reality where the unimaginable became the norm.

The former entrepreneur continues his small-time scams, swindling a woman out of 5.6 million yen ($38,000) by once again promising marriage. When the woman visits the couple with her daughter, Matsunaga takes it upon himself to hold them both captive. Their imprisonment lasts seven months. The two victims later recount enduring tortures similar to those inflicted on Kumio. We'll spare the details. Their ordeal ends when the mother manages to escape by jumping out of a window. She tumbles two stories and runs to the nearest police station.

Futoshi has every flaw imaginable, but he doesn't lack composure. As soon as he realizes the woman has escaped, he immediately releases the daughter and flees yet again, taking Junko, Ren and his two sons (one of whom is a newborn) with him. When the authorities arrive at the apartment, it's empty.

But Junko has had enough. This latest escape has pushed her finally to the breaking point. She reflects on all that Futoshi has forced her to do, from petty financial scams to the grotesque act of grinding the fingers of the real estate agent in a blender. She decides to flee.

Her departure marks the climax of Matsunaga's horrors.

NO POSSIBLE FREEDOM

His sick mind dictates it to him: Matsunaga can only accept one outcome to end his control over another human being—death. Either suicide or one inflicted by hands other than his own. So, what Junko is about to attempt—finally freeing herself—is seen by Futoshi as an unforgivable affront.

The Aum Shinrikyo Sect

The Aum Shinrikyo Cult had as its main goal the establishment of a new world order based on the teachings of its leader, Shōkō Asahara. The sect's objectives were highly esoteric, centered on purifying humanity by destroying the current world and creating an ideal society on its ruins, with Asahara himself at the helm. The cult believed in an impending apocalypse and sought to prepare for what they considered to be the end of the world.

Asahara and the sect's leaders employed various forms of psychological manipulation: restricted sleep, numerous responsibilities and tasks, denial of access to external information, and exposure only to information filtered by the sect.

These extremist beliefs ultimately led to acts of terrorism.

The sect, and particularly its leader Asahara, were held responsible for the sarin gas attack on the Tokyo subway on March 20, 1995, which resulted in the deaths of 13 people and seriously poisoned 6,300 victims. It was also found responsible for the sarin gas attack in Matsumoto in June 1994, which killed 7 people and poisoned 200 others.

Given that the death penalty is still enforced in the Japanese judicial system, Shōkō Asahara was ultimately executed by hanging on July 6, 2018.

April 1997. Junko has left her children with her mother, Shizumi. She lives and works in places she keeps secret. Alone. Understandably so. She is hiding from her former partner, carrying the weight of her complicity with Futoshi on her conscience, and trying to rebuild herself. She has decided to sever all ties with him for good.

Matsunaga goes to Shizumi's home and questions her about Junko's whereabouts. She says nothing and remains resolute.

For the manipulator, this is a failure: his creation is slipping away. The blow is twofold—first to his ego, and second, because Junko might one day go to the police and expose their past. That would be catastrophic for him.

So, Futoshi devises an utterly twisted plan to lure Junko out of hiding: he decides to fake his own death. Three mutual acquaintances, in cahoots with Matsunaga, inform Junko of the father of his supposed suicide. The former teacher, shaken, takes the news hard but also feels an unexpected sense of relief. Without seeking more details about the alleged suicide, she returns to her mother's home.

Of course, Futoshi is lying in wait and confronts her. Junko's brief taste of freedom is over almost as soon as it began.

The torment resumes, and this time, to ensure that his creation never escapes again, Matsunaga extends his control over the entire Otaga family in a manner likened to the methods practiced by the leader of the apocalyptic cult Aum Shinrikyo.

This time, Matsunaga doesn't just shatter the defenses Junko was beginning to rebuild in her mind; he manages to utterly destroy the barriers within every member of the Otaga family. Takashige, the father; Shizumi, the mother; and Rieko, the sister, come to live with Futoshi. He keeps them under his control by threatening to reveal the horrors Junko committed over the years and demands money from them in exchange for his silence—always more money. In Japanese culture, a family's reputation and name are sacred. Thus, the entire family works hard during the day, only to return home in the evening to hand over their earnings to the manipulator. To remove any remaining sense of judgment, he makes them drink, gets them drunk and during these binge sessions, he recounts in detail new crimes, leaving his listeners deeply shaken.

Takashige, Shizumi and Rieko work tirelessly to sustain Matsunaga. They endlessly commute between their jobs, their home and Futoshi's apartment. The lack of sleep takes a severe toll on Takashige, who one evening falls asleep at the wheel and gets into a car accident. Exhausted, the family can no longer provide Matsunaga with enough money. In response, he reverts to his horrific habits, subjecting them to physical abuse and torture using his favored method: electric shocks.

And when it isn't physical attacks, the manipulator assigns tasks designed to further crush the Otagas' spirits. For instance, he gives Takashige a particularly horrific mission: to replace the plumbing in the apartment where Matsunaga and Junko had executed and dismembered Kumio, the real estate agent. Without hesitation, Takashige complies. This serves a dual purpose for Futoshi, strengthening his control while making Takashige an accomplice to the crime by destroying evidence.

From this point, escape becomes unthinkable. Reporting anything to the police is no longer an option. Matsunaga has achieved total mental domination over the Otaga family.

This relentless psychological control and acts of torture shattered the Otaga family to the point where they began to view their tormentor as a prophet-like figure. The methods employed by Matsunaga bear striking similarities to those used by leaders of the world's most sinister cults—a point to which we will return later.

Futoshi even manages to seduce Shizumi, Junko's mother, who falls in love with him, as well as Rieko, with whom he begins a sexual relationship.

By this stage, Matsunaga has no remaining minds in the Otaga family left to break, inhabit or entirely corrupt. That is when Kazuya, Rieko's husband, enters the picture. Kazuya, a former police officer, starts to grow suspicious of his wife's long hours and her nights spent away, often in Matsunaga's bed.

Kazuya accompanies Rieko to Futoshi's apartment and meets a seemingly affable, jovial man who quickly gets him drunk. The former police officer initially finds Matsunaga charming, even entertaining the idea that he could befriend him. He returns, drinks more and begins to lower his guard.

Predictably, Futoshi identifies Kazuya as his next conquest. Slowly, he works to gain control of this "strong mind" as well. Matsunaga, in his usual fashion, shares the most degrading details about Rieko—secrets she had confessed to him that even her husband didn't know. He reveals her past abortion before their marriage and an affair she had with a coworker.

Gradually, Futoshi manipulates Kazuya into turning on his wife and the entire Otaga family. Under Matsunaga's influence, Kazuya begins to insult and physically abuse them, including his wife. Once again, Futoshi delights in their suffering, orchestrating their pain without lifting a finger.

Kazuya and Rieko initiate divorce proceedings, while Matsunaga convinces his new follower to bring Yuki and Aya, the couple's son and daughter, to his residence. Now, six members of Junko's family are living under Futoshi's roof, completely under his psychological control.

Of course, Matsunaga also needs to implicate Kazuya in past crimes, solidifying his grip over him. Using his now standard method of submission, Matsunaga orders Kazuya to the same apartment where the real estate agent was murdered—this time, to replace all the bathroom tiles. Yet another erasure of evidence.

Futoshi has never felt so powerful in his life. He reigns supreme over his "kingdom," having extracted a staggering 63 million yen ($425,000) from the Otaga family. They were even forced to take out loans from multiple banks to sustain Matsunaga's lavish lifestyle.

However, the Otagas are at the brink of financial collapse. Their earnings are now used solely to repay debts. The money supply is drying up, and to Matsunaga, they are no longer useful—or even entertaining.

It's time for Futoshi to move on to the next phase of his life, which means disposing of the Otaga family. But this will require a delicate approach—this time, he is dealing with six people. Eliminating six individuals isn't as simple as getting rid of one or two. Matsunaga knows he must surpass himself to pull this off these disappearances.

He's confident in his intelligence and cunning, but he's acutely aware of the risks. The police are starting to close in on him. Any mistake, even the smallest misstep, could lead to his arrest—or worse, to the death penalty, which the Japanese judicial system still enforces.

The stakes have never been higher for Matsunaga, and the line he walks is razor-thin.

SIX MURDERS BY PROXY: MATSUNAGA'S MACABRE MASTERPIECE

The first to die was the father, Takashige. It was December 21, 1997. His own daughter, Junko, was tasked with torturing him using electric shocks. The man, 61 years old at the time, suffered a cardiac arrest during one of these sessions. The family, horrified, tried to revive him under Matsunaga's disapproving gaze. Their efforts were in vain. He then ordered them to dismember the body and dispose of the parts in public toilets and the waterways of Kitakyūshū.

Did he truly intend for Takashige to die in that manner? It's impossible to know for certain. However, the outcome suited him perfectly. He seized the opportunity, marking the first name off a chilling and macabre list.

The second to die was Shizumi, the mother. This time, it was no accident. Barely a month after her husband's death, on January 20, 1998, Futoshi ordered Rieko and Kazuya to strangle her with an electrical cord. They disposed of her body using the same method as they had with Takashige.

The third victim was Rieko. At 33 years old, she had become completely deaf due to the near daily electric shocks she endured. Matsunaga tasked Kazuya, still married to Rieko, with strangling her, convincing him that he would be ending her unbearable suffering. In the days following this horrific act, Kazuya was overcome with grief, sobbing and repeating, "I can't believe I even had to kill my wife."

He became the fourth victim. His physical and mental health deteriorated rapidly. He began vomiting and defecating throughout the apartment, prompting Matsunaga to lock him in the bathroom. Kazuya ultimately died of starvation on April 13, 1998, at the age of 38.

Now, Futoshi and Junko were the only adults remaining in the group. Matsunaga, the manipulator, ruled over a group of children: Ren—the daughter of Kumio, the real estate agent—Junko's two sons, and Yuki and Aya, the children of Rieko and Kazuya, who had witnessed the brutal deaths of their parents.

Yuki was the fifth to die. The reasons for Matsunaga's decision to target him remain unclear. Although Yuki hadn't been involved in the murders or the disposal of the bodies, the trauma of witnessing his mother's murder and his father's decline had left him deeply scarred. The boy remained silent and immobile for most of the day. In May 1998, Ren held Yuki down on the kitchen floor while Junko strangled him. In an attempt to soothe him, Ren whispered in his ear, "I'll take you to see your mommy." Yuki had just turned five.

Aya was the next to follow, joining her brother, her parents and her grandparents. Her tragic end came on June 7, 1998. Futoshi, fearing that the 10-year-old girl might eventually talk to the police, decided she needed to be silenced. Ren strangled Aya, and in an appalling act of brutality, dismembered her body, boiled some parts, and disposed of them—half in public toilets and the other half in the sea.

It took Matsunaga six months to eliminate the Otaga family, and, of course, he did so without ever lifting a finger himself. He had lost none of his arrogance. However, Futoshi was still unaware that he had made a mistake: failing to orchestrate a seventh murder—that of Ren. The daughter of his first victim would ultimately be the one to bring about his downfall.

REN'S REBELLION

Matsunaga's methods had always proven effective, until now: Ren had been under his absolute mental control for six years. She had tortured, she had killed for him. Why, then, would he think she could break free from his grip?

Yet that is precisely what happens on January 30, 2002. The teenager escapes during a visit to her paternal grandparents' home in Kitakyūshū, who remain completely unaware of her situation. Ren, now 17, has had enough of this unending nightmare. It's unclear whether a specific event gave her the strength to flee or if it was the result of a slow, personal journey to reclaim her freedom.

As expected, Futoshi immediately sets out to find her, but Ren remains elusive. He doesn't give up, interrogating those close to the teenager. It's Ren's aunt who ultimately betrays her by revealing her hiding place to Matsunaga—yet another testament to his frightening persuasiveness.

Matsunaga tracks Ren down and forcibly brings her back to his apartment. She must pay for her attempt to escape. The price promises to be steep. Under Futoshi's stern gaze, Junko pulls out Ren's fingernails with pliers, electrocutes her, and strangles her, stopping just in time to ensure she doesn't die from the ordeal.

These brutal sessions continued until March 6, 2002. Despite being pushed to her absolute limits, Ren finds the strength to escape once more. Determined to see her rebellion through to the end, she takes a shocking step before leaving the apartment: she manages to photograph herself holding her father's heart, which Matsunaga had inexplicably kept.

Why take this revolting photo (the word is fitting)? Because it would serve as undeniable evidence.

Ren returns to her grandparents' home and, this time, she tells them everything. She slams the photo onto the table. Stunned and horrified, Kumio's parents immediately contact the police. It was long overdue.

The next day, March 7, 2002, Futoshi Matsunaga and Junko Otaga are arrested by law enforcement on charges of assault and voluntary acts of torture against Ren. Once in police custody, Ren begins to recount everything, unloading the full, horrifying account of her six years with Matsunaga.

The torture and death of her father, the murders of six members of the Ogata family, and even the unbearable scenes where their bodies were dismembered and discarded piece by piece—all of it comes pouring out.

It's staggering. The police can hardly believe what they're hearing. How could they have missed such atrocities? Why had no one spoken up before her?

Matsunaga must have regretted not deciding to kill Ren when he still had the chance.

The manipulator is finally behind bars. His reign of terror has come to an end, and a trial can now take place. It will confront his unimaginable actions in full. The entire country holds its breath, fearing the worst. The devil is always in the details.

THE TRIAL ALL OF JAPAN AWAITS

The police, however, face a major obstacle: there is no physical evidence to support Ren's testimony. The pipes and tiles in Kumio's apartment had been replaced. Predictably, Futoshi had disposed of Kumio's heart and meticulously cleaned the scene. And how could anyone hope to recover body parts that were discarded years ago into public toilets, ponds, or the sea? To solidify their case, the prosecution needed much more.

It is Junko who ultimately provides the crucial material. On October 23, 2002, Matsunaga's first puppet, now cut off from her master's influence while in prison, confesses. By force of circumstances, the psychological grip he held over her has broken. She tells all and turns against him. She recounts each crime, each act of torture in vivid detail. Much of her account aligns with Ren's testimony, corroborating it.

With her confession, authorities finally charge Futoshi Matsunaga and Junko Ogata with the murders of Kumio, Aya, Takashige, Shizumi, Yuki, Rieko, and Kazuya.

Junko knows she is complicit; she knows she faces serious consequences. Her arrest and the act of speaking out, however, come as twin reliefs. She later admits, outside the official proceedings: "For the first time in twenty years, I can eat, take a bath, go to the toilet freely, and even have time to read." This woman is in prison, potentially for life, possibly awaiting execution. And yet, she feels free. Make of that what you will.

The trial could finally proceed, with the prosecution confident in its case. It began in May 2003 at the Fukuoka District Court. Junko pleaded guilty, admitting her involvement in the crimes. In contrast, Futoshi Matsunaga staunchly maintained his innocence. Had he ever killed anyone with his own hands? Could that be proven? The manipulator wasn't entirely wrong. He declared: "I may have mistreated the victims because I didn't like their attitudes, but what reason would I have to kill them since they were my sources of income?" He blamed Junko, placing full responsibility for the murders on her, as her hands were the ones stained with blood.

However, the court wasn't swayed by Matsunaga's arrogance and attempts to deflect blame. The verdict came late on September 28, 2005. Both Junko and Matsunaga were found guilty of six murders. The court did not classify the death of Takashige, Junko's father, as murder. While the couple was deemed responsible for his death by electrocution, the court found insufficient evidence to prove intent to kill.

The sentence: death.

No murder charges were brought against Ren.

Both convicts immediately appealed to the Fukuoka High Court. However, on September 26, 2007, the court upheld the death sentence for Matsunaga and reduced Junko's sentence to life imprisonment. Explaining the decision, Judge Yasuo Torai stated: "The defendant Junko Ogata had long been under the physical and psychological control of the defendant Matsunaga, and her involvement in the crimes was therefore subordinate." Junko's nearly spontaneous confessions and her consistent expression of regret throughout the trial also played a significant role in the court's decision.

In stark contrast, Matsunaga remained unrepentant. Throughout the proceedings, he displayed no remorse and offered no apologies for his numerous victims.

Undeterred, Matsunaga filed another appeal with Japan's Supreme Court, arguing that he could not be sentenced to death since he had never personally killed anyone. In 2011, the country's highest court rejected this final appeal, bringing the legal battle to an end.

Today, as I finish writing this chilling account, Futoshi Matsunaga awaits execution by hanging in a prison cell.

How can one grasp the hold that this man exerted for so many years over such a large number of individuals, driving most of them to commit unspeakable, atrocious, and sordid acts?

Futoshi Matsunaga had a knack for charm, presenting himself as affable and sociable—at least at first. This allowed him to identify the weaknesses of his victims, which he would then exploit to his full advantage. He coupled this with the threat of physical violence, readily demonstrating his capacity for brutality to further solidify his control.

He meticulously regulated every aspect of his victims' daily lives, from their sleep schedules to mealtimes, keeping them entirely under his control and reducing them to mere puppets. Stripped of their autonomy, they became hollow reflections of themselves, ready to follow Matsunaga's every command—even to the point of committing murder against their own family members.

It was a relentless psychological machinery at work.

We must commend the extraordinary strength of Ren, whose courage, after years of suffering, finally brought an end to the actions of this truly unique serial killer.

LUCIE BLACKMAN, THE MISSING HOSTESS

I'VE ALWAYS HAD a restless spirit, an insatiable desire to travel. It's been with me for as long as I can remember. . . The thrill of discovering another country, sometimes even another civilization, new customs; talking to people with perspectives different from my own; savoring dishes I've never encountered before.

I've been fortunate to explore many different countries, and every time, I've returned richer—spiritually and as a human being. For me, traveling is a dream.

It was the same for Lucie Blackman.

But dreams can sometimes turn into the most harrowing of nightmares. That's what happened to this young and curious free spirit.

On February 9, 2001, in a seaside cave on the Miura Peninsula—a lush coastal area about 30 miles (50 km) south of Tokyo—police made a horrifying discovery. Inside the cave, they unearthed plastic bags containing human body parts. These remains had been placed in a bathtub—yes, a bathtub—that was buried inches 2 feet (60 cm) deep. The body had been dismembered into eight pieces. The head was shaved and encased in concrete. Due to the advanced decomposition, authorities could not determine the cause of death. Eventually, forensic experts identified the victim through dental records. It was Lucie Blackman, missing for more than seven months.

My aim here isn't to discourage you from pursuing adventures in far-off places. No, I wouldn't dream of doing that. But Lucie's story serves as a sobering reminder to be cautious. This is her story.

THE LOVELY LUCIE

First and foremost, let's meet Lucie Blackman. Born on September 1, 1978, in Sevenoaks, a picturesque countryside town in Kent, southeast England (the same region you pass through when taking the Eurostar to London!), Lucie Jane Blackman was the eldest of three children. Her father, Tim, and mother, Jane, were overjoyed when they welcomed their first child into the world. Everything seemed perfect in their little family until a terrifying incident occurred when Lucie was just 21 months old.

Tim vividly recalls the horrifying night when he was jolted awake by a scream from Jane—one of those heart-stopping cries that etches itself into your memory forever. It was a sound that haunted him.

"Lucie was lying motionless at the bottom of the bed, and she felt clammy," Tim recounted. "I picked her up and laid her on the floor. She was turning gray, a sickly black-gray color. It was clear that her heart was no longer pumping blood through her body. I didn't know what to do—I thought she was going to die."

Jane frantically called emergency services, but Tim could see that seconds mattered. Lucie's mouth was tightly shut, and he wasn't sure if she was even breathing. He forced her mouth open and discovered that she had literally swallowed her tongue, preventing air from reaching her lungs. Without hesitation, Tim acted. To the immense relief of both parents, Lucie began to breathe again, and her skin regained its healthy, rosy color.

The paramedics later explained that Lucie had experienced a febrile seizure—a muscle spasm caused by fever and dehydration, which had caused her to swallow her tongue. Without Tim's decisive action, Lucie could have died within minutes. From that night on, Lucie always slept with a light on. Interestingly, her name, Lucie, comes from the Latin word lux, meaning "light." A fitting name, indeed.

Far from deterring them, this terrifying episode only strengthened Jane and Tim's desire to have more children. They couldn't bear the thought of losing Lucie and being left without children. It was an unthinkable prospect.

Soon, Lucie's sister, Sophie, and her brother, Rupert, were born. The Blackman family thrived, living a happy and vibrant life in their home near Granville School. Lucie, a diligent and serious student, brought laughter to her classmates and teachers alike with her razor-sharp sense of humor. Jane, who had endured a difficult and somber childhood after losing her mother at an early age, made it her mission to foster harmony and joy within the family. She was the glue that kept their happiness intact.

Until the first shadow darkened everything. It was 1996, and Lucie was not yet 18 years old when the fairy tale came to an end. Tim had cheated on his wife. It was just a fleeting affair, but Jane couldn't bear it. She filed for divorce and was granted custody of their three children. From then on, Lucie moved into a small brick house located in a disadvantaged area of Sevenoaks.

The place felt dismal to Lucie, who found the rooms too dark. Moreover, the house had been the site of a tragedy: the previous owner, who had mysteriously disappeared, was later found buried in a nearby town, murdered by his former lover. (I should add this case to my little list. . .)

Despite all these negative aspects, Lucie always considered this house her final home. It must be said that the young woman had a strong sense of responsibility as the eldest child. The presence of her brother and sister eventually brightened the place. She became like a second maternal figure to them, taking on the role of mediator in family conflicts.

Lucie is now a beautiful young woman, tall, blonde, with blue eyes. She could talk about anything, and people always listened to her with rapt attention. Her mother, Jane, used to say: "If Lucie starts telling you the story of a sugar cube, you can be sure it will be the most fascinating story you've ever heard!"

She remained a diligent and hardworking student while being outgoing, which made her popular with her peers. She even earned a scholarship to attend Walthamstow Hall, a very prestigious private school. However, unlike most of her classmates, Lucie didn't plan to apply to university after passing her GCSE (General Certificate of Secondary Education, the equivalent of a high school diploma in England, usually obtained around the age of 16). No, Lucie was passionate about travel and exploring the cultures of other countries. What she really wanted was to seize her youth by traveling, exploring the globe, and discovering new civilizations.

But Lucie wasn't one for backpacking. Hiking or traveling with just a sleeping bag and a rucksack wasn't her style. She preferred spending time in the bathroom taking care of her hair, painting her nails, or standing in front of her closet deciding which pair of high

heels to wear. So how could she reconcile her love for travel with her taste for elegance?

The answer was clear: Lucie decided to become a flight attendant. It was a glamorous profession. She applied to British Airways, and after just 21 days of training, she was hired! It was May 1998, and Lucie was only 19 years old!

After two years of service, the dedicated Lucie earned a coveted promotion sought after by many flight crew members: assignments on intercontinental flights to more exotic destinations. Now, she had the opportunity to travel to America, Asia, and Africa.

While Lucie was initially delighted with her new rotations, her enthusiasm soon began to wane. Exhaustion set in. Her sister described that challenging period of Lucie's life: "Lucie could be in Paris in the morning, Edinburgh in the afternoon, and then head to Zimbabwe the next day. She was so exhausted from the time differences that she couldn't enjoy anything during layovers—not even the food."

The young woman who wanted to see the world ended up seeing little more than hotel rooms in major cities, all of which started to look the same.

Let us now introduce, if you will, Louise Phillips into our story. She is Lucie's best friend. The two had known each other since the age of 13. They shared the same passions (notably for makeup), the same way of speaking, and the same mannerisms. They were like two soulmates. Louise also worked at British Airways.

The two young women had spent a lot of time together ever since their teenage years. It was Louise, who was also growing weary of her job, who came up with an idea that might initially seem far-fetched or even downright odd.

What if they both went to Japan, to Tokyo, to become. . . hostesses at a bar!?

Louise's older sister, Emma, had told her about this fabulous metropolis and its wonders.

This suggestion intrigued Lucie. Hadn't she dreamed of discovering another civilization without needing to carry a backpack? Tokyo, the most populous city in the world with its 14 million inhabitants, was a dream destination. Emma assured them that they

Bar Hostesses in Japan

In Japan, a hostess bar is a type of nightlife entertainment establishment where women, known as "hostesses," interact with male customers by offering companionship, engaging in pleasant conversations, and sometimes participating in board games or artistic activities. These bars aim to create a relaxed and friendly atmosphere where customers can escape the stress of daily life and feel valued by the attention of often young and attractive women. Hostesses are usually dressed according to the theme of the bar. Their primary role is to converse with customers while encouraging them to order drinks. This latter aspect forms the basis of most of their earnings.

could earn a lot of money working as bar hostesses while enjoying the pleasures of the capital.

It must be said that Lucie is in desperate need of money. She is living beyond her means, with £7,000 in revolving credit to repay to her bank, and debts piling up after she cut off her income. On the verge of depression, Lucie makes a drastic decision: she resigns from British Airways. This happens in mid-April 2000.

She leaves her family a somewhat vague farewell letter, in which she doesn't explicitly mention her future job but hints at it with her usual sense of humor.

> *"My best friend, Louise, is going to Tokyo to stay with some relatives, and the opportunity came up for me to go too. I don't have any specific plans once I'm there—maybe explore the culture, learn the language, or become a high-class, well-paid geisha!!! (Just kidding)*
>
> *Just a break for a few months, something different—they say a radical change can be as healing as rest."*

Lucie confided only in her mother, and, to be honest, Jane immediately felt that this move to Japan was a very bad idea. She would later recount, years afterward:

"Lucie kept reassuring me—she would never do anything reckless, she would be very careful. But I had this feeling that something horrible was going to happen to her. I just couldn't get it out of my head. I had never thought of Japan before, as a place. But as soon as she said the word—Japan—a voice came to my mind, saying, 'Something terrible is going to happen.'"

Other family members and several of Lucie's friends shared the same sense of unease. They struggled to understand her sudden decision to travel more than 5,600 miles (9,000 km) to a country completely unfamiliar to her, one that didn't particularly interest her and whose language she didn't speak.

Jamie Gascoigne, her new boyfriend, was the most upset about the matter. After all, Lucie and he had been discussing getting engaged soon. And now, she wanted to end their relationship to travel to the other side of the world with her best friend? But why?

In the weeks leading up to her departure, Lucie's behavior changed. She became withdrawn, a stark contrast to her usual openness with others. On the flip side, she began reaching out to reconnect with family members she had lost touch with—her godfather, cousins, uncles, and aunts—and most notably her father, with whom she had severed ties after the divorce. At home, she started throwing away clothes, old letters, and personal belongings. "Out with the old, in with the new!" seemed to be her motto. Her mother grew worried: why was her daughter getting rid of all these things if she was only going to Tokyo for a few months? It was almost as though Lucie had a premonition that she would never return home...

From that moment, Jane did everything she could to dissuade her daughter from leaving and tried to convince her to stay in England. She even considered hiding Lucie's passport, an ultimately futile plan since Lucie could easily have a new one issued. Moreover, Jane didn't want to make her daughter angry—she didn't want Lucie to leave for Tokyo upset with her. That would have been the last straw. So, without telling her daughter, she took on the role of a guardian angel and scattered healing crystals she had purchased online into Lucie's suitcase as a form of protection.

On the morning of May 4, 2000, Louise's mother drove her daughter and Lucie to Heathrow Airport, the largest in the United Kingdom. This time, the two friends would board without wearing uniforms, seated among the passengers rather than standing in the plane's aisles. Just before boarding, Lucie answered a call from Jamie, her ex-boyfriend, who made one final attempt to persuade her to stay in Britain. He later recalled: "She had gone too far, past the point where she could turn back. She couldn't turn to Louise and say, 'Look, I can't go.' So she told me, 'I'm on the steps; I have to go.' Then she boarded and left." The plane took off for Tokyo, and Lucie flew toward her fate.

THE MYSTERIES OF TOKYO

Lucie arrives in Japan twelve hours later, accompanied by Louise. The two friends have a ninety-day tourist visa to rely on as they try to secure employment at a hostess bar. Upon arrival, Lucie seems somewhat disoriented—a mix of fear and excitement. In her journal, which will later be discovered, she writes just minutes after landing:

> *It's 9:13 a.m. here in Tokyo, which makes it half past midnight in England. I'm sitting on my suitcase in the subway, feeling completely overwhelmed. I'm so tired, scared, anxious, lost, and utterly drenched in sweat too! I hope that, looking back, I'll laugh at my naivety—the way I had no idea what was waiting for me.*

The reaction of the young Englishwoman isn't all that surprising, truth be told. Lucie had just left Sevenoaks, a town of 100,000 residents, for a sprawling metropolis of extraordinary density. With its suburbs included, Tokyo boasts a population of 30 million—half the total population of the United Kingdom! She must have felt as though she had stepped into an alien world, so vastly different from anything she had ever experienced before.

I had the chance to visit Tokyo a few years ago. It's hard to put into words the impression one gets upon arriving in this astounding city. It's truly another world—everything is so different! Tokyo is a city that never sleeps. Things are happening at all hours. Everywhere in the streets, there's life, lights, giant billboards, 24-hour shops, references to manga and popular series. And, most strikingly, this sense of strangeness is heightened by the fact that very few Japanese people speak English fluently. Unlike in the West, English isn't a commonly spoken language in Japan. You find yourself on your own in a country where most of the locals can't understand you.

Where would the two young women settle? Before their departure, they had told their families they would be staying with Louise's Japanese aunt (the wife of her mother's younger brother). But Lucie's mother never believed in this economical solution, and she was right to be skeptical. In reality, Emma, Louise's sister, had booked a room for the new arrivals at Sasaki House. "House" sounds like a hotel with clean rooms equipped with comfortable beds. Imagine their astonishment when, after a long and exhausting journey by plane and train, Lucie and Louise found themselves staying in a place known as a gaijin house.

Gaijin Houses
A guesthouse—or "gaijin house," which means "house of foreigners"—is a type of inexpensive accommodation for foreigners in Japan. In many cases, the low cost and constant turnover of tenants, including backpackers, street vendors, and night workers, meant that gaijin houses were dirty, unsanitary, and far from comfortable.

In a testimony collected after the incident, Louise described the house near the Tokyo Olympic Stadium where they moved: "It was disgusting. We were really in shock. We looked into the living room, and there were two people stoned on the couch. They were smoking joints. The room smelled. You could barely make out the inside because of the smoke."

The tiny room that the two friends had to share had only one small window, without a curtain, overlooking the concrete wall of the neighboring building. The futon mattress wasn't even equipped with sheets. The mirror was cracked, and the toilet (Turkish-style) and the bathroom were filthy.

From their first night, Lucie and Louise came up with the perfect nickname for their guesthouse: The Shithouse. In the following days, they did their best to turn their room into a more livable space by decorating it with posters, postcards, and scented candles, and installing curtains on the window.

It was only the day after their arrival, after having slept most of the following day due to fatigue, jet lag, and the heat, that the two best friends headed toward the Roppongi district.

The Roppongi district is known as one of the wealthiest areas in the Japanese capital. It boasts several Michelin-star restaurants, some of the most beautiful museums in the country (and even the world), as well as numerous boutiques from the world's top luxury brands. But it's also a lively district with many vibrant bars and clubs that stay open late into the night, attracting foreign businessmen and wealthy, party-loving tourists.

Of course, Louise and Lucie didn't end up there by chance. This is the district where they are most likely to find work in a hostess club. But their tourist visa prohibits them from working. So, they cannot simply show up at a club's front desk with the best intentions. No, they'll have to be clever.

It was more like providence—though, in hindsight, perhaps providence isn't quite the right word—that approached the two young women on the street, in the form of a young, handsome Japanese man. The man, who speaks English, approached them and asked if they were looking for hostess work. He was influential and could introduce them to club managers and help with their job search. Unsure at first whether to trust this stranger, Lucie and Louise, feeling intrigued, ultimately agreed to follow him to a small nightclub, the Club Casablanca.

This bar is nestled in a brown building with simplistic architecture, which also houses one of the largest strip clubs in Tokyo: the Seventh Heaven. While you can't ignore the Seventh Heaven, you could walk past the building a thousand times without even noticing the Club Casablanca.

To access it, you must climb to the sixth floor of the building. Upon entering, you find yourself in a dimly lit room where the host will greet you and guide you to one of the available tables before signaling an hostess to begin entertaining you. It's the typical set-up for a bar in the area, though at Club Casablanca, unlike other establishments in the Roppongi district, it is not allowed for the hostesses to offer sexual services to their clients.

Here, the hostesses—mostly foreign girls—are there to sit, smile and flatter the clients, while encouraging them to drink and spend as much money as possible. However, they were free to work outside the club by offering dōhan to clients (paid dates, usually around dinner or karaoke).

After answering a few simple questions from the English-speaking manager of Club Casablanca, Lucie and Louise are hired on the spot. Just a few days after arriving in Tokyo, the two friends start working six nights a week, from 9 p.m. to 3 a.m., for a monthly salary of about 300,000 yen ($2,000), which means Lucie was earning a few hundred pounds more than her salary as a flight attendant at the time. But it is the bonus system that truly allows the hostesses to become wealthy. If a client requests to be entertained by a particular person, or if they order an expensive bottle, the hostess will receive an extra payment. With the dōhan, it's not too difficult to earn a bonus of $800 per month. However, if the hostesses fail to secure more than fifteen dōhan per month, they're fired. The competition is tough, but Lucie and Louise are already familiar with this kind of selection from their time at British Airways. They're motivated and ready to rise to the challenge.

Lucie immediately feels at ease in her new job and gets off to a good start by earning the trust of a regular club patron, Ken, who comes to see her every night she is working during the first two weeks, without exception. Similarly, Louise quickly racks up dōhan and becomes very comfortable in the parties and drinking sessions of the Tokyo nights, which continue at a fast pace.

However, Lucie begins to feel an unhealthy pressure. She compares herself to Louise and feels at a disadvantage. Private requests for meetings keep coming, and she struggles to fulfill them. Additionally, she realizes that the rent for Sasaki House, the cost of renting her bike, and the other living expenses in Tokyo drain all of her hostess earnings. She had hoped to pay off her debts by working like crazy, but that plan is failing! Burnout is once again on the horizon. Three weeks after her arrival on the archipelago, Lucie writes in her journal:

> *Lucie's feelings in her journal reveal the intense emotional turmoil she's going through. The pressure and stress are taking a toll on her self-esteem, and the comparison to Louise, who seems to be thriving in the environment, is exacerbating her sense of inadequacy. The debt, combined with the feeling of being trapped in a situation she's not equipped to handle, is overwhelming. Despite being surrounded by her best friend, she feels isolated and deeply unhappy, struggling with self-hate and the exhaustion of trying to meet expectations.*
>
> *Would you like to explore further or continue with the story?*

Lucie does not yet realize that her writings are prophetic and that, in less than two months, she will indeed disappear. And this time, for eternity.

VAPORIZED!

As often with Lucie, periods of doubt and depression are followed by more joyful moments. After writing the previous lines in her journal, Lucie regains her energy, and her attitude becomes positive again. Her condition slowly starts to improve. It is during this time that she begins dating Scott Fraser, an American Marine stationed in Tokyo. Scott has a genuinely positive impact on Lucie, helping her regain confidence. At the Club Casablanca, the clients can tell; the young hostess becomes increasingly popular and regains her status as one of the favorites of the establishment, just like in the beginning. The requests for dōhan start pouring in.

On July 1, 2000, just two months after her arrival in Japan, Lucie agrees to a private appointment that will have immensely heavy consequences. Strangely, she does not communicate the name of the client to Louise, as she usually would. On the afternoon of the first of July (it was a Saturday), the young woman receives a call from her mysterious client on the public phone booth at Sasaki House. He informs the hostess that he will be a little late and that he will call her back when he is near the Sendagaya station, their meeting place. It is the day off for the two friends, and they are very happy to be going out together. It is agreed that Lucie will call Louise at the end of her appointment with the mysterious client to set a common meeting point.

Lucie then leaves the guesthouse. This is the last time Louise will see her alive. Here are the events of that evening as they unfolded from Louise's and Scott's perspectives:

— At 5 p.m., Lucie contacts Louise from the public phone at the guesthouse using the client's mobile phone and informs her that he is going to take her to the seaside.

— A few hours later (Louise doesn't remember the exact time), Lucie calls her friend again, this time from her own line. The client had just given her an expensive phone. She tells her best friend that they also shared a bottle of Dom Pérignon, one of the world's most expensive champagnes (about $250 a bottle). Lucie confirms that she will be back at the guesthouse in about an hour at the latest.

— Immediately after, Lucie calls Scott, but he doesn't answer, so she leaves him a message saying they will meet tomorrow for lunch.

Everything seems to be going well.

But Lucie, an hour later, still hasn't returned to the guesthouse. Her absence worries Louise, who knows her friend to be punctual. And then, why not call her if she's late? Louise rushes to the Club Casablanca to inform the manager and her colleagues. They shrug it off. Well, so what? Lucie may have decided to "go the extra mile" and spend the night with her client. After all, if he's a handsome guy. . . But Louise knows her best friend too well to believe this is likely. Lucie is not an easy girl, and she would never fall into the depths of prostitution.

Louise spends a sleepless night searching for her best friend in the bars and clubs of Roppongi, but of course, her efforts are in vain. Is Lucie still by the seaside with her client? She also calls local hospitals and clinics with the help of a colleague who speaks Japanese, but no one reports the arrival of an English woman matching Lucie's description. Feeling helpless and increasingly worried, Louise thinks about notifying the local authorities, but there's a small problem—Lucie and she are working illegally on the island. Telling the police about the situation would only add a new problem to the one they already have. She decides to wait until Sunday.

In vain. Lucie still hasn't returned. So, Louise has no choice but to go to the Azabu police station in Roppongi on the morning of Monday, July 3, to report her friend's disappearance.

But the police show little interest in Lucie Blackman's disappearance. At this point in this tragic story, Louise's interlocutors treat the disappearance lightly. They will soon regret this. To them, it is not unusual for a Westerner to leave Tokyo for a few days or continue their travels without necessarily informing their loved ones. First reason. Then, Lucie is an adult, 21 years old, and she had every right to do whatever she wanted. Second reason. And the third reason, not the least: in the Japanese mindset, leaving a job as a flight attendant for one of the most famous airlines in the world to become a hostess in a bar in the Roppongi district is seen as proof that the person lacks judgment. So, she could have simply left Tokyo on a whim, right?

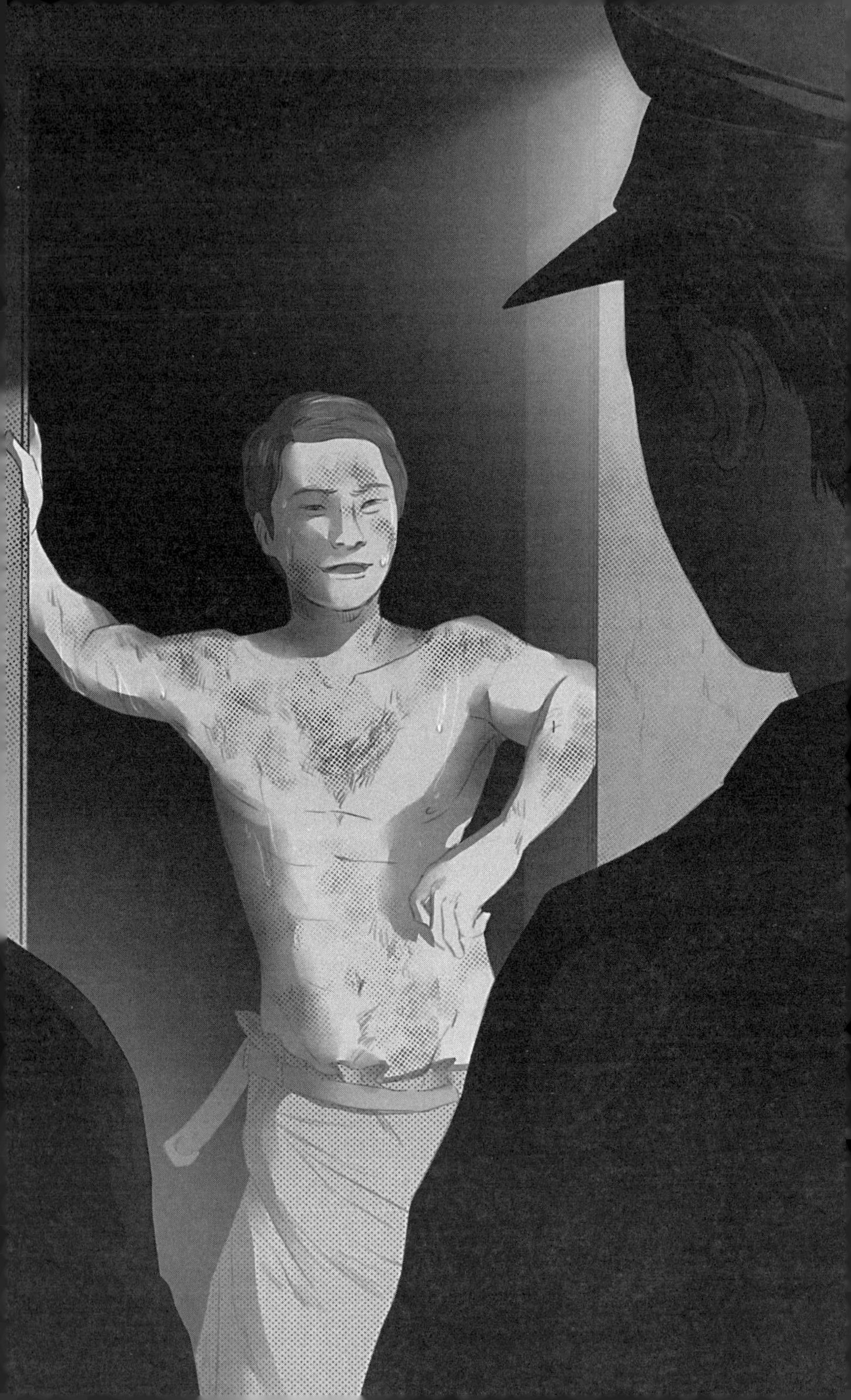

As we can see, Louise receives no help from the police. But the Englishwoman doesn't give up and goes to the British Embassy in Tokyo. After meeting with the vice-consul, she recounts the events of the past days, and the official seems genuinely concerned. He calls the highest-ranking officer at the Azabu police station to express his worry. However, this does absolutely nothing in practical terms. Unfortunately.

That same Monday afternoon, an event happens that will escalate Louise's anxiety to its peak. At 5:30 p.m., she receives a call for her on the public phone at Sasaki House. Her mysterious caller speaks English with a very strong Japanese accent. He says his name is Akira Takagi and claims to be calling on behalf of Lucie Blackman. In a calm and almost friendly voice, Akira tells Louise that her friend is doing very well.

"I am with her in our 'dormitory.'"

Louise asks to speak with her.

"She can't right now. She's studying and practicing a new way of life since we met. She has so much to learn this week. She can't and doesn't want to be disturbed."

Akira provides some details about Saturday's events. Louise does her best to get him to talk.

"Lucie came back to the Sendagaya station after her appointment on Saturday. Then, she crossed paths with my guru. He impressed her so much that she immediately decided to follow him and join his religious cult, the Newly Risen Religion, based in Chiba city, about 30 miles (50 km) west of Tokyo."

Louise is stunned. Who is this guy? He's clearly making things up. She asks again to speak with her friend.

"Lucie isn't feeling well and doesn't want to talk to anyone right now."

Then, this time, he abruptly hangs up. In disbelief, Louise looks at the small silver handset she's tremblingly holding in her hand. But as soon as she hangs up, it rings again. On the other end of the line, Akira again: "I'm sorry, the signal must have been cut off. Lucie can't speak to you right now. She isn't feeling well. Maybe she'll call you at the end of the week. But she has started a new life and won't be coming back. Don't count on it. I know she has a lot of debt, 6,000 or 7,000 pounds ($7,750-9,000), but she will repay it somehow, don't worry about that. Anyway, she just wants you and S'kotto (the Japanese version of Scott) to know that she's doing well. And that she's planning a better life, away from the world."

Louise is in shock. She feels that Akira's explanation for her best friend's disappearance makes no sense at all—this story about a guru, a retreat... But her anxiety heightens as she is frightened to realize that this man, whoever he is, knows everything about the young woman—even the name of her boyfriend and her financial problems. Louise insists once again to speak with Lucie. Akira then ends the call, saying, "I'm sorry. I just had to let you know that you won't see her again. Goodbye." At that moment, Louise thinks that indeed, the likelihood is high that she will never see Lucie again... alive.

THE INVESTIGATION FINALLY BEGINS

This alarmingly unsettling call convinced Louise to do what she had been hesitant to do since Saturday night: inform her family of Lucie's disappearance. After all, why should she cause her relatives, who were 5,600 miles (9,000 km) away in England, to panic over what could merely be a temporary runaway? But now, with Akira's strange and incoherent statements, everything had radically changed. She made the call she had been dreading.

The following events unfold in Sevenoaks, England. Jane Blackman is at home, coincidentally preparing a package of sweets for Lucie when she receives Louise's call. She is immediately plunged into a whirlwind of panic and fear. Not only has her beloved daughter disappeared in a distant country she knows nothing about, but it is Akira's chilling words that freeze her blood.

She immediately calls for her two other children, Sophie and Rupert, and contacts Tim to inform him of their daughter's disappearance. It's the first time they've spoken since the divorce.

Sophie, determined, is accompanied by her boyfriend Jamie. They immediately suspect a criminal disappearance—whether it's intuition or a sixth sense—and suggest flying to Tokyo the next morning to oversee the search efforts.

Once in the Japanese capital, Sophie and Jamie shuttle between the British Embassy and the Azabu police station in Roppongi but can only observe the police's indifference to helping them find Lucie. This frustration builds up.

Sophie then discusses with her father, who is still in England but on high alert, the possibility of making Lucie's disappearance public. Not only in Japan but also in England. Someone must have seen or noticed her on the day she disappeared. . . A public appeal for witnesses seems to be their last resort in trying to gather information about the young woman, as the police remain indifferent. However, this carries a risk: if Lucie is in the hands of a kidnapper, he may panic and end up killing her. A cruel dilemma.

In the end, the Blackman family won't have to make that cruel choice. Emma Phillips, Louise's older sister, who is in love with Japan, goes to The Daily Telegraph, one of the largest British daily newspapers, to tell them the entire story of Lucie. Without even asking the family for permission. It's bold. It's incredibly bold. But her audacity pays off. Within a few days, the disappearance of the 21-year-old woman is widely covered in the British media, including on the internet, in the press, on TV, and on the radio.

In every report, journalists emphasize the negligence, or rather the total apathy, of the Tokyo police. They are right. This case took place eighteen years before the case of Tiphaine Véron, and it is sad to note that nothing has changed on the Japanese side regarding the disappearance of Westerners. . . But that's another story.

Desperate by the situation and feeling too far from the scene of operations, Tim Blackman arrives on the Japanese archipelago on July 12, 2000, to help Louise and his daughter's boyfriend. He immediately joins the search and holds press conferences to request information about Lucie. He holds the conferences with his arms raised, holding a photo of his daughter in his hand. "Every piece of information could prove crucial. . . I implore you to speak up if you know anything. . ."

For the whole family, as well as for Louise, it is unthinkable that Lucie suddenly joined a religious cult, or that she fled to avoid paying her debts. They are convinced, along with the press and public opinion, that Lucie is being held against her will by a kidnapper. In the best-case scenario.

The increased media attention, coupled with the pressure from Tony Blair, the British prime minister at the time, and Robin Cook, his foreign minister (who's visiting Tokyo), leads the Japanese authorities to finally open a criminal investigation into Lucie Blackman's disappearance.

A few weeks later, on August 1, 2000, the police receive a typewritten letter, supposedly from the missing young woman. The full contents of the letter have never been made public, but it's said to have ended with the following words:

I do what I want, so please leave me alone.

The short letter was signed with Lucie Blackman's name, but Tim, her father, didn't recognize his daughter's signature at all. The letter was also full of linguistic and grammatical errors that suggested it hadn't been written by a native English speaker, indicating it was just a hoax. It was pathetic.

However, at the same time, testimonies begin to flood in about Lucie now that the Japanese police are taking the investigation seriously. It turns out that the young Briton may not have been the first to be taken to the seaside by a well-dressed, wealthy man who spoke excellent English. A man who arranged his meetings at Sendagaya Station.

Three women shared a similar story with the police: they had all woken up with pain and sickness in an unknown man's bed, with no memory of the previous night. Where? By the sea, in the city of Zushi. The police cross-reference the names of known sex offenders who might live in Zushi, on the waterfront. And then, bingo! A name comes up in the files. And not just any name. . . Joji Obara, 48 years old. Quite the background, this guy.

The call for witnesses had been crucial. In chess, it would

be considered a masterstroke. The difference is, on our very real chessboard, Queen Lucie is already checkmated. So. . . who is this Joji Obara?

JOJI OBARA

Joji Obara was born in Osaka under the name Kim Sung-jong on August 10, 1952. His parents were Zainichi Koreans.

The Zainichi
They are descendants of Koreans who came to settle in Japan during the occupation of Korea by Japan, particularly during World War II.

The Japanese term "Zainichi" literally means "who remains in Japan" and is used to refer to both kankokujin (from South Korea) and chosenjin (from North Korea). The term can be used to describe any person (even non-Korean) who resides in Japan without Japanese citizenship, but it is most commonly used to refer to Koreans.

Zainichi Koreans still face discrimination today due to the racism present in Japanese society.

Obara's father was a wealthy real estate developer. Obara inherited properties and then amassed a fortune by heavily investing in real estate, only to go bankrupt and lose everything during the 1990s recession. Afterward, to recover, and because he couldn't help but live a lavish lifestyle, Obara used his business as a front to launder money for the Yakuza Sumiyoshi-kai, one of the branches of the Japanese mafia. And this was just the beginning of Joji Obara's criminal activities.

Obara was a heavy drug user and truly a despicable man, especially towards women. He was arrested in 1998 after attempting to film women in public restrooms. It was thanks to this conviction that the police were able to identify him as a potential suspect, following the accounts of other women. Even though they did not know the man's real name and couldn't recall the exact address where they had woken up, a simple glance at the list of individuals with sexual offense records living in the seaside apartment complex area in Zushi led the police to Joji Obara.

THE INVESTIGATION ACCELERATES

The Japanese police, with this lead, finally had something to work with. They discovered that Obara had indeed traveled to Tokyo on the day of Lucie Blackman's disappearance. Had this vile man taken the young hostess to his place, and if so, what had happened to her? It was then that the police, to their great dismay, realized they had visited Obara's home under strange and troubling circumstances five days after Lucie Blackman's disappearance.

The manager of the Blue Sea apartment complex, located on the Miura Peninsula, 20 miles (32 km) from Zushi, had called the police because of unusual noises coming from one of the apartments under his supervision. When the officers arrived that day, they were greeted by Joji Obara, shirtless, covered in sweat and concrete dust. While he allowed the officers into his hallway, he categorically refused to let them search the entire apartment without a warrant (in Japan, as in the United States, and unlike in France, a judge's warrant is required for police to enter private property).

Fine. A man could very well be carrying out noisy renovations in his apartment, couldn't he? At the time, the police had no reason to suspect anything sinister was happening: Lucie's disappearance had not yet made the headlines. In this case, the police completely mishandled things, from the beginning almost to the end.

Of course, in light of Lucie's disappearance, this episode was seen in an entirely different light and hastened the criminal's arrest. While the authorities did not yet have enough evidence to arrest Joji Obara in connection with Lucie Blackman's disappearance, they were able to detain him for five counts of rape following reports from other women. Now, judges had issued arrest warrants, and the police were free to search Obara's numerous properties across Japan. The task ahead was daunting. Very daunting indeed.

Joji Obara's main residence was filled with chaos: piles of clutter, old car batteries, broken televisions, receipts, newspapers and personal recordings dating back to the 1970s. In a large freezer in the basement, police found the frozen body of a German shepherd. Obara later explained that he had preserved his beloved pet in the hope that one day, science would allow him to clone the animal and bring it back to life.

Authorities also found the numerous diaries kept by this criminal. In them, they read his deep-seated hatred of women, with entries along these lines:

> *Women are only good for sex. I will lie to them. I will seek revenge. Revenge on the world.*

But it was the more than 400 video recordings that revealed the true nature of the monster Joji Obara was. In these harrowing videos, which Obara secretly filmed without his victims' knowledge, he is seen with women—always unconscious—whom he sexually assaulted while wearing nothing but a Zorro mask.

In his journals, painstakingly analyzed by the police, Obara referred to it as a mere "game of conquest," a euphemism he used to describe what he had done to all these women. Over 200 names were found in the pages—200 names of women assaulted between 1983 and 1995. Further along, he even admitted to having no sexual interest in conscious women during his assaults. His modus operandi was always the same: Obara would contact a hostess and take her to his home, where he would offer her a drink laced with a powerful tranquilizer. Once his victim was unconscious, he would begin to assault her. Cross-referencing the video tapes with entries from his diaries suggested that between 200 and 400 women fell victim to this criminal. Obara didn't kill his victims; they would escape from his apartment, traumatized but alive, often refraining from pressing charges to avoid the stigma their families might impose. But at least two hostesses were not as fortunate.

When authorities reviewed the video footage, they came across a tape showing Obara with an unconscious woman—Carita Ridgway, a 21-year-old Australian model. She had worked in Tokyo's Ginza district as a bar hostess until her sudden death on February 29, 1992, after being rushed to the hospital, where she was declared brain-dead. And who was the person who brought Carita to the hospital, claiming she had food poisoning from eating seafood? Joji Obara, of course. In Obara's journals, police found the true explanation for the model's sudden death:

Carita Ridgway, too much chloroform.

Obara had offered to take Carita home and then attempted to drug the hostess with chloroform—his usual, well-practiced method. Forensic pathologists had no difficulty piecing together the sequence of events. By using too much of the toxic liquid, Obara caused acute liver failure, which led to her brain death. Carita passed away in the hospital after life-support systems were turned off at her family's request.

And still, no investigation followed her death. Earlier, we mentioned two hostesses who were not fortunate enough to leave Joji Obara's apartment alive. The second, tragically, was Lucie Blackman.

THE DEATH OF LUCIE

The police found no diary entries from the murderer concerning Lucie, nor any video material showing Obara with the young Englishwoman. However, after a meticulous search of his apartment in Zushi, forensic technicians discovered strands of long blonde hair. DNA analysis confirmed that they belonged to Lucie. Authorities also uncovered two photographs of her posing on Obara's balcony, along with receipts for the purchase of a handsaw, a chainsaw, and plastic bags in the days following her disappearance. It was hard to believe Obara was preparing to chop firewood for the winter. Few purchases could be more incriminating. Yet, despite this overwhelming evidence, Obara continued to deny any knowledge of Lucie's disappearance.

At this point in the investigation, the only pressing question—and the one that plunged Lucie's family into utter despair—was: Where is the young woman's body?

With no cooperation from the suspect, the police pressed on with their intensive searches across Obara's numerous properties and surrounding areas.

Finally, on February 9, 2001, almost seven months to the day after Lucie's disappearance, they made the macabre and tragic discovery described earlier. Lucie's body had been dismembered into eight pieces, her head shaved and encased in concrete. The killer had placed everything in a bathtub and buried it at the bottom of a cave. The absolute horror.

On April 6, 2001, while still in custody for the rapes, Joji Obara was formally charged with the murder of Lucie Blackman. The task now was to bring him to justice.

THE TRIAL

It began just three months later but stretched over several years. What made the prosecution's task challenging was the lack of direct evidence linking Obara to Lucie's death; they had only circumstantial evidence.

Here is a comprehensive list:

— It was revealed that on July 2, 2000, the day after Lucie's disappearance, Obara called a hospital to ask how to resuscitate an overdose victim.

— A few days later, police visited his apartment after neighbors complained about unusual noises.

— A receipt found at Obara's home showed he had purchased a chainsaw, cement mix, and other tools from a hardware store. However, while the autopsy suggested Lucie's body had been dismembered with a chainsaw, the tool in question was never found.

— Police discovered Lucie's hair in Obara's apartment, but no DNA evidence was found on her body directly linking her death to Obara.

Another factor further complicated the image of the Blackman family. Toward the end of the trial, Tim Blackman accepted a "condolence payment"—a settlement of $580,000—from a friend of Obara's and subsequently questioned the validity of the evidence against the suspect. Jane, outraged at even being offered money, rejected a similar offer outright.

To defend his actions, Tim explained that the money was used to support his family after their tragic loss and to establish the Lucie Blackman Trust, a foundation aimed at raising awareness among young people about staying safe while traveling abroad.

After six long years of legal proceedings, on April 24, 2007, Joji Obara was found guilty of eight charges of rape and manslaughter in connection with the death of Carita Ridgway. But, to everyone's surprise, Obara was acquitted of the murder charge in Lucie Blackman's case. Judge Tsutomu Tochigi justified his decision by stating, "There is no evidence that Obara was involved in her rape and murder. The court cannot prove that he was involved in her death."

What was clear was that Lucie and Obara had been together before her disappearance, but there simply wasn't enough forensic evidence to establish a direct link between their encounter and Lucie's death. While Joji Obara was sentenced to life in prison for multiple counts of rape and manslaughter of Carita Ridgway, the Blackman family was not satisfied with the verdict. Understandably, they appealed, and a new trial began in 2008. This time, the outcome was different.

In December 2008, the Tokyo High Court overturned Obara's acquittal and convicted him of the abduction of Lucie Blackman. He was also found guilty of drugging and raping her, as well as dismembering and disposing of her body. While there still wasn't enough evidence to prove that Obara had murdered Lucie, it was clear that he was responsible for the mutilation of her body. A partial victory, perhaps, for the Blackman family—but a victory nonetheless.

Throughout this time, Obara maintained his initial claims to preserve his innocence, never admitting to being a rapist and murderer who had destroyed the lives of hundreds of women.

Today, Joji Obara is serving a life sentence for the abduction of Lucie and the disposal of her body, as well as for the death of Carita Ridgway.

THE FLAWS THAT THIS TRAGEDY REVEALS

The Lucie Blackman case deeply impacted public opinion in both Japan and the United Kingdom. It raised awareness about the exploitation of young women, mostly foreigners, who work—whether legally or illegally—as bar hostesses in Japan. This tragedy also exposed flaws in the police force—remarkably slow, only launching its investigation at the last minute—and in the Japanese judicial system, particularly in criminal matters.

The complete lack of regard for victims means that they often don't report rapes, fearing they will be labeled liars and even rejected by their families, or worse, by society as a whole.

It was later revealed that other women had reported waking up in Joji Obara's bed after being drugged and sexually assaulted. However, for years, these reports were either silenced by the victims or ignored by the authorities.

There is no need to rewrite history here. But one can argue that if Obara's many victims had not hesitated to file complaints, if they had been listened to, and if an investigation had been launched immediately following Carita Ridgway's death, perhaps Lucie Blackman would still be alive today.

MASUMI AND HER KILLER CURRY: DINNER OF DEATH

The image of an ordinary person going off the rails. . . the kind, family-oriented mother, the jovial neighbor, the grandmother who goes shopping at the same time every day, the well-organized, upstanding office worker. . . Is this a stereotype in criminal cases? Should we assume that we are all potential murderers, that our impulses can be awakened in any of us following a single event or by a series of repeated incidents? I am not a psychiatrist, and even the most eminent specialists would be hard-pressed to easily answer this question.

Are psychopaths born, or do they become so? Are there mental barriers in many of us that will prevent us from ever acting on our impulses, no matter what happens? And for others, is there a possible primary loss of these protections that will inevitably lead to an act of violence?

Do "born monsters" truly exist? Or does one become one after experiencing terrible childhood traumas, and then continue down that path in later life?

A vast question. I'm not sure the answer can be found in this shocking case of Masumi Hayashi. But it may offer some avenues for reflection. The breakdown of an ordinary mother for a cause. . . Well, you'll read for yourself.

Every summer, hundreds of colorful and extravagant festivals called *matsuri* take place across Japan to celebrate the new season. *Matsuri* are intended to allow people to thank the Shinto deities, forget the worries of daily life for a few days, and maintain the communal spirit in their villages or neighborhoods. Moments marked by peace and joy. . . with one exception.

It's 1998, in the village of Sonobe, in Wakayama, next to the large university in the city. It's 75°F (24°C), the air is mild, and the sky is a clear blue, as it typically is during this season on this part of Honshu Island. Wakayama is a calm port city, located about 300 miles (500 km) west of Tokyo. The *matsuri* in Sonobe village is in full swing: people are singing, dancing, food is sizzling, and sweet aromas are wafting over the tables. Then, suddenly. . . participants begin to collapse one after another. No gunshots are fired. No. They clutch their stomachs, roll on the ground, and faint. It's not one, two, or three villagers who fall. . . it's dozens. . .

THE TRAGEDY

Let's return to the matsuri of Sonobe village. . . It's July 25, 1998. Almost every town and village in Japan has its own traditions, some of which go back centuries. Each one has its own way of organizing its matsuri. Sonobe's matsuri is particularly renowned: parades featuring magnificent floats honoring the deities, streets beautifully decorated, organized games, musicians and dancers performing all over at any time. . .

But, in Sonobe more than anywhere else, attention is paid to the food. It has to be a true feast for the taste buds of the participants. Japan is often considered a paradise for food lovers because of the combination of simplicity and complexity, unique ingredients, and rich flavors offered by Japanese cuisine. During summer festivals, food stalls called yatai offer a variety of delicious traditional dishes, such as yakisoba (stir-fried noodles) and takoyaki (dumplings made from pancake-like batter containing pieces of octopus), as well as curry.

The famous curry of the Sonobe summer festival. People come from far and wide to taste it! It may surprise some that curry, originally from India, is actually extremely popular in Japan and considered a central part of national culture. However, instead of being aromatic and spicy, the Japanese version of the dish (which no Indian would recognize) is generally mild and sweet: a very popular, comforting food introduced into the country by British naval officers in the late 1800s. Japanese curry consists of rice, curry sauce, vegetables (usually onions, carrots, and potatoes), and meat (pork, chicken, or beef).

In Japan, an adult eats curry more often than other dishes typically associated with the archipelago, such as sushi and tempura, because it is an easy and quick dish to prepare, in less than an hour, unlike other dishes that require long cooking times.

Shintoism and Its Main Deities

Shintoism (in French "the way of the gods") is an animistic and polytheistic cult practiced by the majority of Japanese people, venerating the forces that animate nature. It was "created" to unify various ancient beliefs and distinguish them from Chinese Buddhism.

It is difficult to pinpoint the exact official birth of the Shinto religion in Japan. It is considered that its rise coincides with the appearance of Japanese civilization, during the prehistoric Jomon period, roughly between 13,000 and 400 B.C.E.

Shintoism is unique in that it does not rely on any founding myth or official sacred text. Its priests offer very little guidance. Their main duties involve maintaining the sanctuaries and conducting ceremonies. Among these are the matsuri and annual processions, where puppets representing the deities, or kami, are carried. Everything that can be thought of or experienced is linked to different kami, and the key is to live in harmony with them. There are said to be nearly eight million deities in this religion! Anything can be honored: rocks with strange shapes, waterfalls, and, of course, primary elements such as the sun, earth, rain, and wind.

The kami, unlike Western gods, have moods like humans and are capable of both good and bad actions. Good and evil are not opposites, and a deity can shift from one to the other during its existence. Shinto sanctuaries are considered resting places for the kami and thus serve as places of worship for the Japanese. They can be found as easily on street corners in large cities as in remote forest clearings.

Among the principal kami, there are:

— Izanagi and Izanami, who represent the co-creator couple of Japan and are also twins. From the floating bridge of heaven, they stirred the ocean with a celestial spear. The salt drops that stuck to the spear formed the first piece of land of the archipelago, which today belongs to the island of Awaji, in the Kansai region. They settled there and decided to marry, which gave birth to the other islands of Japan as well as countless kami (deities);

— The sun goddess, Amaterasu, emerged from the left eye of her father when he purified himself in a river. Amaterasu is the most revered deity in Shintoism, and the national flag, the Hinomaru, which symbolizes a red circle of the sun, directly refers to her;

— Inari, the deity of good harvests in a country where rice cultivation is so important. She is one of the most popular and widely represented kami in Japan. In most religious sites, one encounters statues of a fox named kitsune, which is Inari's sacred animal messenger.

All of these deities, these kami, have been portrayed in the animated films of Hayao Miyazaki, from Studio Ghibli, who continues to depict them with great sensitivity and poetry.

All you need to do is buy a curry sauce or curry roux. They are sold in block form and can be found in any grocery store in Japan. Holding up okay? Is your stomach not growling too much? If you're hungry, you might want to satisfy it now, because in a few pages, you won't have the same appetite. . .

Let's continue.

After the lighting of the Japanese lanterns at 6 p.m., festival-goers of all ages spread out across large tables to enjoy the much-anticipated curry. Most of them decided to eat on the spot, while others only nibbled, saving the curry for later, at home, in order to keep a taste of the matsuri and extend the moment of joy and togetherness.

That night, Megumi Kagawa, 34 years old, devours her serving. She is the daughter of the couple who owns the land where the festival is held. She wouldn't miss it for the world. Megumi finds the curry delicious, perhaps just a bit too spicy for her taste. She then heads home, full, and happy with her colorful memories and the traditional music still ringing in her ears. But soon after returning home, Megumi begins to feel a vague nausea. Then her stomach starts to contract in horrible spasms. She screams. The curry comes back up. The young woman vomits violently. A neighbor, alerted, peeks inside and delivers some alarming news: all those who ate curry at the festival dinner are showing symptoms of food poisoning. Adults and children alike—sixty-seven people in total—are suffering from nausea, spasms, and abdominal pain. Some, even after vomiting the contents of their stomachs, continued to writhe in pain on the floor.

At the matsuri site, it's a scene of chaos. There is indeed a private clinic located about a hundred meters from the festival, but only one doctor is on duty that evening and is quickly overwhelmed by the situation. Ambulances must be called, and the poisoned victims—especially the children—need to be transferred as quickly as possible to other hospitals in Wakayama. Emergency services are handling the dispatching. The faces of these men and women, accustomed to emergency situations, leave no doubt: they grimace, they are worried. For the symptoms to have arrived so quickly after the curry was consumed, it is clear that this is not a minor issue, not just a piece of spoiled meat, for example.

As the public health center of Wakayama begins to suspect a mass food poisoning, it quickly becomes apparent, due to the scale of the events, that something much more sinister, much darker, has occurred during the summer festival. The police are called to the scene. The hours pass in frantic concern for the families of the poisoned victims.

In the night, at precisely 3:03 a.m., Takatoshi Yanaka, 64, the president of the residents' association, dies. Then it is the turn of

vice president Takaaki Tanaka, 53, as well as Miyuki Torii, 16, a first-year student at the private Kaichi High School, and later in the night, Hirotaka Hayashi, a young boy. He was only 10 years old. Thanks to the determination of the emergency responders and medical teams, by the time the sun rises again over the archipelago, the sixty-three other victims—several of whom had been admitted to the hospital with life-threatening conditions—are considered to be saved. They will not lose their lives.

The doctors, who are able to breathe a little after this nightmarish evening, then speak with the police. For them, there is no doubt: this is not a case of food poisoning, but rather nothing less than. . . poisoning. Cyanide is suspected, given the symptoms.

Rumors spread. At the site of the matsuri, devastated by the parade of emergency responders, festival-goers gather, utterly incredulous. How is this possible? Someone would have deliberately poured one of the most toxic poisons in the world into the curry? It's a terrifying thought that some refuse to even consider. Why would someone want to poison, blindly, dozens of people, including children?

As the Wakayama Prefecture Police establish their headquarters at the Higashi police station, near the city's large park—the closest to the festival site—to begin their investigation, autopsies are urgently performed on the four deceased, and the remaining curry is, of course, analyzed by the forensic laboratory teams.

In the blood and stomach contents of the four victims, it's not cyanide that is found. . . but another substance, also highly toxic, another terrifying poison: arsenic.

Everything depends on the dose, though, because your body, like mine, contains arsenic. This is the issue with this substance, which naturally occurs in the earth's crust and is distributed throughout the environment—air, water, and soil. But while it is possible to be exposed to arsenic through contaminated water, whether drinking it or using it to prepare food, this exposure typically does not result in death within hours. It usually takes years of exposure to contaminated groundwater for the health effects of arsenic, including skin lesions, to appear. For a person to experience immediate symptoms of arsenic poisoning, such as vomiting, abdominal pain, severe diarrhea, along with tingling in the extremities and muscle cramps, they must have ingested a large quantity of the substance all at once.

Returning to the analysis of the curry, when the dish served at the Sonobe summer festival is tested by toxicologist Hiroshi Yamauchi, it is found that the sauce contains 6 mg of arsenic per gram. 300 mg of the poison is considered the lethal dose for an adult. This means that eating only 1.5 ounces (43 g) of the sauce would almost certainly result in death. So, poisoning did indeed occur. And as a result, there is a poisoner.

For the police, the investigation has now taken a turn: they are dealing with a criminal case. Regardless of the identity of the murderer, it is clear that they intended to make as many victims as possible. What made this idea so terrifying was the fact that the killer didn't know who would eat the curry or who would opt for the yakisoba noodles instead.

What did this suggest? That the poisoner was targeting a specific individual, someone they knew and were sure would choose the curry for dinner. . . And if that meant sacrificing innocents to conceal the crime, so be it. This was one possibility. The second possibility was that the poisoner simply wanted to cause as many deaths as possible at the festival, blindly, without targeting anyone in particular. The only thing that mattered was to kill as many people as possible, both children and adults.

Which of these scenarios chills you the most? Personally, both do.

The case quickly makes the headlines in Japan. As the press floods the festival site and journalists seek answers to their questions, the authorities send several envoys, such as Shogo Kakimoto, the representative of the social department of Wakayama, who declares on the evening of the tragedy:

"It wasn't about hatred toward any particular individuals. Anyone could have eaten from the curry pot, there could have been hundreds of people poisoned. It's so hard to believe that a human being could do something like this. . . A random massacre." Kakimoto has chosen his side. Was he right to do so?

Let's continue the investigation, shall we? Who prepared this poisoned curry?

The authorities provide an update. More than twenty volunteers, mostly local housewives, combined their skills to make the curry. Cooking started around noon in the garage of one of the festival organizers and continued until 3:00 p.m., when the mixture was poured into two large pots and moved to the festival site. In the garage, investigators easily find the container of the weapon of the crime: a blue paper cup placed on a shelf near the pot, containing about 35 milligrams of arsenic at the bottom.

During these three hours, the cooks took turns overseeing the curry's cooking and ensuring it stayed at a boil, a critical step to making the dish.

Twenty cooks, twenty suspects. A game of Clue in the kitchen. Each of them, since they were alone at the time, could have mixed the arsenic powder into the large pot.

While the police continue their serious investigation, they decide to cancel all other summer festivals and events scheduled in the region to ensure that a similar tragedy doesn't occur again, because there is no way they are taking any risks if there is indeed a "serial poisoner" on the loose.

At the same time, rumors are circulating in the town about the presumed identity of the assassin: people are naming names without any evidence and flooding the press with outlandish theories, which are promptly denied by the police.

Megumi Kagawa's parents—owners of the property where the festival was held—are the first to be suspected, even though their own daughter could have also lost her life. The festival took place in their yard, and the Kagawas did not participate in the celebrations. Furthermore, the Kagawas run a pancake restaurant in town and could have easily had access to the curry during its preparation. Some people are so sure of the couple's guilt that they forcibly break into the restaurant to ensure there is no arsenic in the okonomiyaki batter, the Japanese pancakes they sell. The rumors are ugly. . .

Those less affected by the poison begin to leave the hospital rooms. They've escaped a horrific death, but that doesn't mean they won't suffer long-term consequences. The doctors warn them: lifelong headaches, facial swelling, heart problems, severe rashes, and generalized weakness. The community is incredulous: who could have committed such an atrocity?

Then, a testimony will turn everything upside down and direct the investigators' suspicions toward a particular name. When questioning eyewitnesses who were around the house where the curry was prepared, the police record several testimonies regarding the suspicious behavior of Masumi Hayashi, a 37-year-old woman who was part of the cooking team and had stayed near the pot for nearly forty minutes. More importantly, Masumi was seen acting very strangely when entering the garage. She checked her surroundings, looked both ways, and appeared very agitated. One witness even recalls her holding a sort of blue cup in her hand. Remember. . . Investigators had found a blue paper cup near the pot in the garage, containing traces of arsenic.

But that's not all. The authorities immediately begin investigating Masumi Hayashi's past, scanning her life. . . Many troubling things will soon come to light.

PROFILE OF THE SUSPECT

Who is she? Who is this woman from the neighborhood who volunteered to help prepare and oversee the making of the curry, with the likely intention of adding a touch of arsenic and thus decimating her community?

Born on July 22, 1961, in a small fishing village south of Wakayama city, Masumi Hayashi is the daughter of a fisherman and an insurance agent. Aside from that, we know very little about Masumi's upbringing. She left no lasting memories with anyone, and her own family had little social interaction outside of close relatives. After high school, she began training to become a nurse in Osaka, where she met her future husband, Kenji, during her second year of

study. Kenji, an exterminator (interesting, right?), is sixteen years older than Masumi, and when their relationship began, he was married with no children. Madly in love with his young mistress, he quickly divorced. In 1983, Masumi and Kenji got married. They would have four children: one boy and three girls. Tired of her nursing career after a few years, Masumi decided to quit and followed in her mother's footsteps by becoming an insurance agent. In 1995, three years before the matsuri tragedy, Masumi and her family moved to Sonobe into a large house with a huge garden, by a stream. A beautiful spot, a comfortable place to live. Yet, the Hayashis rarely received neighbors, nor were they invited anywhere, and they made no effort to integrate into the community.

The couple is rather well-known for hosting mah-jong parties, a Chinese-origin board game, with friends from outside the village. It's as if Masumi wanted to avoid any contact with her neighbors. She wouldn't even let her children play with the local kids. Needless to say, the residents of Sonobe didn't view this behavior very positively. That's an understatement. In a country like Japan, especially in small villages, it's expected that each family integrate into the community and participate in its functioning. Masumi's deliberate choice to stay apart was seen as an act of arrogance by her neighbors, a sign of selfishness, and some even believed it reflected a kind of malice.

But it wasn't just Masumi's behavior that raised eyebrows. The townspeople also found the Hayashi family's lifestyle odd. Something wasn't quite right. The family owned a brand-new BMW and didn't hesitate to parade it through the village streets. They lived in a property valued at around 70 million yen, which is over $475,000. But how was this possible? Kenji had retired from his pest extermination job shortly after moving to Sonobe, and Masumi's salary as an insurance broker didn't reach staggering heights. So how was the couple financing their lifestyle and mah-jong parties, during which, it would later be revealed, large sums were gambled? Patience, patience. . . Everything eventually comes to light. And the tragedy at the festival will allow the police to give a clear and definitive answer to this question.

In the meantime, the police investigation can continue. And it would be perfect if the investigators could shift into higher gear. Everyone is eager to know if Masumi is truly guilty.

THE INVESTIGATION

Thus, thanks to eyewitness statements, the police knew that Masumi had the opportunity to mix the arsenic into the curry sauce. But can these testimonies really be trusted? The Hayashi family is not well liked in Sonobe. . . Could some people have taken the opportunity to settle scores? To dig even deeper into the couple's lack of likability? This hypothesis lingers in the minds of the police.

Of course, when she is arrested and "interrogated" about it, Masumi becomes defensive and denies any involvement in the case. She asks what her motivation could have been to commit such a heinous act.

Indeed, traces of arsenic trioxide powder are found in the basement of the family home. But Kenji Hayashi had worked as an exterminator, so he had access to various arsenic-based pesticides, including those needed to get rid of ants. This is not conclusive proof.

"It doesn't make any sense for a mother of four children who works hard, as you would agree, Officer, to try to poison my entire neighborhood, including innocent children, by adding poison to curry. . . You don't believe that, do you?"

The theory may seem far-fetched, indeed. However, Masumi Hayashi is the only suspect the police have, and as soon as her name is thrown into the media, journalists launch a full-fledged witch hunt. They have material to work with. Kenji, Masumi's husband, testifies:

"There were guys trying to steal our mail from our mailbox or climb onto our roof to photograph the inside of our daughter's room. When I complained that their actions were crossing the line, one of them responded and said, 'Well, my boss said that to get a scoop, they'll tolerate breaking the law because I can get away with a suspended sentence.'"

It's cynical, perhaps. But it's the truth. The atmosphere eventually deteriorates to the point where the Hayashis become prisoners in their own home, surrounded by journalists 24/7. The constant pressure and stress of knowing they are being watched in every little action become increasingly difficult for the couple and their children to endure. Especially since, aside from the visual testimonies, there is no solid evidence to support Masumi's guilt. In this context, it is not surprising that one day the mother of the family feels the need to fight back. While photographers snap photos of her watering her garden, she begins to spray them while shouting at them. The images, which later loop on every news channel, are brutal. They show a woman at her breaking point, and people read into this rather harmless gesture as clear proof of her guilt. In any case, no one wants to consider her innocent. She can cry her innocence in several interviews, but it doesn't matter. Masumi Hayashi is an poisoner, a witch of the worst kind.

As sociologist Hikaru Tanaka later explained:

"The entire nation became convinced she was guilty. I don't see how anyone could have thought she was innocent, given how she was presented in the media."

The police continue their investigation without wanting to draw attention to themselves. It is only on October 4, 1998, months after the curry poisoning, that the police finally arrest Masumi and Kenji Hayashi. Thirty police officers go to the couple's home to inform them of their arrest. Hundreds of journalists follow the scene, filmed live. But the most surprising aspect of this arrest is the reason behind it: insurance fraud and attempted murder.

Two distinct cases from the previous one that open up Masumi's psychological abyss and will allow it to be fully explored.

BUSINESS WITHIN THE BUSINESS

Let's return to the origin of the Hayashi couple's fortune. If it intrigued the neighbors, there's no doubt it raised even more questions for the investigators. So, they combed through the family's accounts, followed some leads, and pulled many strings. The solution to this mystery came quickly: Masumi had used her knowledge of the insurance sector to receive compensation based on false claims. These included exaggerated accidents; for example, Masumi claimed to have suffered a serious bicycle accident that left her unable to work, while in reality, she had merely burned herself with hot oil while cooking. Meanwhile, her husband Kenji reported a serious motorcycle accident, even though he had simply fallen down the stairs. And this was just a small part of the long list. By the time the authorities realized the Hayashis had been persistently committing fraud, the couple had scammed various insurance companies out of 160 million yen, equivalent to more than $1.1 million! This was the first reason for their arrest.

Now, the second reason. The police traced an incident that occurred in June 1997, about a year before the festival tragedy. A tenant who had rented a room from the Hayashis suddenly fell gravely ill and had to be hospitalized. His insurance paid the full medical expenses plus a premium. It turned out that Masumi had pocketed the 5 million yen (about $34,000). But what really caught the investigators' attention was why the tenant had been admitted to the emergency room. You guessed it, right? Poisoning with arsenic!

One could argue that the person might have been accidentally exposed to arsenic. Did he tamper with the cellar where Kenji stored his old chemicals? Or was he deliberately poisoned to collect even more money? In light of the massive poisoning at the festival, the most credible explanation is clearly not an accident. And as the investigators dug even deeper, they were in for more surprises. . . The couple, through their lawyers, reaffirmed their innocence and obtained their release. But this wouldn't last long for Masumi.

On October 26, the insurance agent was arrested again for yet another fraud accusation. . . along with a new attempted murder charge. Another acquaintance of the Hayashis had been hospitalized after dining with the couple in March 1998. It later emerged that Masumi had taken out a life insurance policy on this person, and once again, traces of arsenic were found in the victim's hair. There was no more doubt. This was a clear modus operandi. In the weeks that followed, more and more accusations piled up. But each time, Masumi was released due to lack of tangible evidence.

On November 18 of the same year, the cases resumed. This time, even Masumi's fiercest supporters were outraged: Masumi was suspected of having poisoned her own husband in February 1997 after setting up a life insurance policy. There were now testimonies from close friends coming to light. Some of Masumi's friends claimed she had spoken for years about poisoning her husband and collecting the insurance money. But Kenji survived the attempt, even though it seems the aftermath of this incident led him to stop working and apply for retirement benefits.

Thanks to this accumulation of cases, the police now had certainty that Masumi Hayashi could be behind the tragedy at the festival. However, the investigators still faced a challenge in obtaining concrete evidence to directly link the prime suspect to the murders. They examined the poison itself more closely, leaving no stone unturned. Their idea was to track every trace of arsenic around Masumi. According to a forensic analysis report, arsenic oxide was found in eight different locations: inside a paper cup found at the crime scene, on the inner surface of a plastic container in the Hayashi family's kitchen, in three containers (one capable of holding more than 110 pounds/50 kg of food), in a brown Tupperware container belonging to Masumi's brother, in a milk container in the old Hayashi house and, of course, inside the various pots containing the curry. Quite the charming inventory, wouldn't you agree?

This time, the police left nothing to chance. They requested a very thorough analysis of the poison. Using the Spring-8 machine located in the city of Sayo, which uses synchrotron radiation (employed by Japanese manufacturers for material analysis and biochemical protein characterization), the arsenic samples were analyzed and compared to each other. Based on the specific impurity quantities, it was concluded that the arsenic oxide found in the paper cup was identical to 100% of the arsenic powders discovered in Masumi Hayashi's house.

The authorities went even further by requesting the analysis of the main suspect's hair. The prestigious St. Marianna Medical University in Tokyo performed the analysis using atomic absorption spectrometry. The results were quick to arrive: a sufficiently high level of arsenic was found in her hair fibers to suggest that she had handled the poison (she had likely inhaled minute amounts), even though she had never ingested it. Scientific evidence, the strongest of all evidence, right?

Based on these conclusions, Masumi Hayashi was finally arrested on December 9, 1998, for murder and attempted murder in the Sonobe festival case. She was accused of mixing arsenic into the curry pot. Despite all the mounting and damning evidence, Masumi continued to claim her innocence. Her stance was clear: why would she commit such a heinous act? The police were still stuck on the motive, it's true. But that wouldn't stop them from bringing Masumi Hayashi to trial in the Japanese courts.

THE TRIAL, AND BEYOND...

The long-awaited trial of Masumi Hayashi begins on May 13, 1999. On the first day of this trial, which is called "sensational" by the entire Japanese press, over 5,000 people are waiting outside the Wakayama District Court to try to witness this legal moment. The entire nation is still shocked by this horrific crime, and many citizens want to be present for every twist and turn.

It's not about the suspense regarding the verdict, no. Among those accused of serious crimes in Japan, 99.9% are found guilty. Unlike in France, trials are held without a jury, and the defendant's fate is left in the hands of a panel of professional judges, who are often stern. The main concern here is whether Masumi Hayashi will be sentenced to... death.

Despite all the evidence, she has maintained her denials and proclaimed her complete innocence. After months of interrogation and media pressure, she never confessed to the poisoning. However, the prosecution is confident it can do without her confession: they have prepared about 1,700 pieces of evidence that they are ready to present during the trial. This trial will last three and a half years. It's immeasurable. In France, few trials last more than three months of hearings.

Based on eyewitness testimonies, the Wakayama Prefecture police have reconstructed the tragedy minute by minute, explaining how Masumi brought arsenic powder into the curry using a paper cup and then mixed the poison while she was alone with the pot in the garage. According to the prosecution, no one else had a similar opportunity that day. Masumi was seen pacing angrily near the garage, and, furthermore, she is the only woman who participated in the cooking of the curry who did not fall ill. This argument makes an impact.

But as convincing as the prosecution's arguments are, the evidence against Masumi was purely circumstantial. Does the prosecution have any conclusive, verified evidence? That remains to be seen. Even if the arsenic found in the paper cup matched that at the Hayashi home, it's not truly conclusive, as most of the arsenic in Japan is imported from the same production factories in China.

A plot twist strikes the prosecution hard during the trial, much to the delight of the defense. One of the key eyewitnesses, whose testimony was crucial for identifying Masumi, retracts during the trial, describing a woman with longer hair and different clothes than Masumi was actually wearing that day.

A scientific expert specializing in poisons testifies for the defense, claiming that the traces of arsenic found in the defendant's hair could have simply been from the curry's steam, meaning the curry could have been poisoned before Masumi watched over it.

Then the prosecution faces what has struck us from the beginning of this story: how can the motivations of Masumi be convincingly explained? What is the motive?

The motive! It's crucial in a criminal case. Decisive. You follow me, and I've said this often, right? Here, what is the motive?

Indeed, Masumi Hayashi admitted that she was prone to "fits of anger" and pleaded guilty to the insurance scams in which arsenic had been used. An absurd rumor spread in the press during the trial, claiming that Masumi had taken out life insurance policies on the people present at the festival in order to collect payouts after their deaths. How ridiculous. . . First, she would need their signatures. And how could she have known for certain that these people would choose the curry that night and consume enough to die from it? Poisoning the entire village and committing a massacre didn't make much sense for mere financial gain.

The prosecution also argued that the summer festival tragedy could have been an act of somewhat deranged revenge: Masumi may have wanted to teach the community a lesson because she felt that the people of Sonobe had avoided her and her family. However, it turns out that it was actually the Hayashi family who had refused to integrate.

Others believe that Masumi may never have intended to kill anyone but simply wanted to "make people's stomachs hurt." However, the amount of arsenic mixed into the curry was so large that this hypothesis doesn't really hold up.

The judicial process was so lengthy that, a year and a half into the trial, Masumi began showing signs of nervous depression. In May 2000, she was placed under special surveillance after swallowing three 3-centimeter-long metal nails she had managed to extract from the broom she used to clean her cell. Did Masumi attempt to commit suicide? In the end, she only sustained minor injuries to her throat. Once she was declared out of danger, the trial was able to continue.

In the same year, in October 2000, Kenji Hayashi was found guilty of three counts of insurance fraud. Masumi admitted during her husband's trial that she had been the mastermind behind these scams, at least she was honest about that, which led the prosecution to request a slightly lighter sentence for Kenji. In the end, he was sentenced to six years in prison. To conclude Kenji's story, he served his sentence at the Shiga prison and was released on June 7, 2005.

We must now bring this interminable trial to a close. It would be exhausting, and frankly uninteresting, to detail the entire court proceedings. Finally, on December 11, 2002, the verdict was delivered: Masumi Hayashi was found guilty of three counts of attempted murder, three counts of insurance fraud, and four counts of murder by poisoning. She caused the deaths of four people, including two children.

The judges' decision was based on the following points:

1. The arsenic mixed into the curry was the same as the one found in the defendant's home.
2. A high concentration of arsenic was also detected in the defendant's hair fibers, which indicates she had frequently handled this poison.
3. On the day of the summer festival, the defendant had access to the curry and, according to testimonies, acted strangely throughout the preparation of the dish.

When it was time to pronounce the sentence, the presiding judge of the court, Ikuo Ogawa, declared:

"The four victims were suddenly deprived of their lives during a summer festival they should have enjoyed, and they were in no way at fault. It is entirely natural that their grieving families demand that the accused be severely punished."

As requested by the prosecution, Masumi Hayashi was sentenced to death by hanging for her crimes. Upon hearing the cruel verdict, Masumi, who had remained calm throughout the trial, jumped from her seat and protested vehemently, maintaining her claim of innocence.

Masumi's lawyers immediately appealed the case to the Osaka High Court. The president rejected the appeal in 2005. A further appeal was made to the ultimate jurisdiction, the Supreme Court. The same conclusion was reached on April 21, 2009. Chief Judge Kohei Nasu specified:

"The fact that the motive was not clarified does not affect the conclusion that the defendant is the perpetrator of the crime. The examination results and indirect evidence have proven that the defendant is guilty."

Indeed, the mystery of the motive remains unresolved.

Masumi Hayashi's final request to annul her death sentence was rejected on May 18, 2009, and the death penalty was confirmed the following day after her last attempt to avoid execution.

At that point, with no further appeal attempts, Masumi Hayashi became the eleventh woman sentenced to death in post-war Japan and one of the few women in her special unit who was also a mother.

From that moment, Masumi had no other choice but to present new compelling evidence to seek a review of her trial and avoid being hanged. Continuing to maintain her innocence, she persisted and requested a new trial in Wakayama District Court on July 22, 2009, arguing that the arsenic analyses conducted by the National Research Institute of Police Science and Spring-8 were unreliable. Supported by independent studies, she argued, with the backing of her lawyers, that the method used by Spring-8 was not precise enough for forensic analysis. She also highlighted the fact that the School of Medicine at St. Marianna University in Tokyo had used an outdated method to analyze her hair. Instead of a computerized system, the institution had used a 1970s-era atomic absorption spectrometer and still relied on paper and pen recorders that detected arsenic based on pH levels. The details aside, according to her lawyers, it would appear that the arsenic in Masumi's hair was not above the levels that anyone could naturally have in their hair. After all, everyone is exposed to trace amounts of arsenic through their ordinary diet. Arsenic is an element in the periodic table, an undeniable fact. But in reality, this was merely a set of scientific arguments, the last chance defense.

Masumi Hayashi had already poisoned people with arsenic before the festival tragedy and had even pleaded guilty to insurance fraud. Even though the evidence against her was not truly perfect and the motive was still unclear (a simple act of revenge against the community? Or a manifestation of psychopathic behavior?), no other suspect had emerged in the case. What were the chances of another person using the same substance to poison the curry that Masumi helped prepare? Nearly none, let's be honest. . .

Ultimately, Masumi's first request for a new trial was rejected in March 2017.

Then came June 9, 2021. On that Wednesday, Hayashi submitted another request. Was she doing it to redeem herself in the eyes of her family? Probably. But it was all in vain. On the same day, a terrible event occurred: one of her daughters, aged 37, committed suicide by jumping from a bridge at Kansai International Airport while holding her four-year-old daughter in her arms. But that wasn't all: another granddaughter of Masumi, the eldest daughter of her eldest daughter, aged 16, died that same day, apparently as a result of physical violence from her parents. Three more deaths, and not minor ones.

On January 31, 2023, a year and a half after losing three close relatives, Masumi's second request for a new trial was rejected by Wakayama District Court. A few days later, on February 2, 2023, Masumi Hayashi filed a new appeal with the Osaka High Court and is currently awaiting a decision at the Osaka Detention Center, where she is held on death row. Through her lawyers, Masumi stated:

"There is a real culprit out there. I'm determined to prove my innocence and do everything I can to find them."

THE PLEA BOOK BY HER SON KOJI HAYASHI

In August 2020, Masumi's son, who goes by the pseudonym Koji, published an autobiography in which he states clearly that he is not at all convinced that his mother is the killer behind the curry pot. In his book, Koji makes several shocking claims, stating that Masumi had been beaten during her interrogations, that her children were shouted at if their testimonies contradicted the conclusions of the police, and that Kenji, his father, had learned from the investigators that his wife had cheated on him while the detectives were trying to get him to sign the divorce papers.

Additionally, Koji provides elements regarding a potential new culprit. He mentions that as a child, he had heard stories about a man who poisoned pet dogs in Sonobe. No one is able to identify this person, nor even confirm if he truly existed or if it was merely a local urban legend. Koji clearly remembers that his father said the dog poisoner must have been the one behind this horrible crime. But can these testimonies be taken at face value? More generally, Koji wonders. . . Were the evidence against Masumi sufficient to sentence her to death?

In an interview following the publication of his book, Koji takes the opportunity to describe the conditions in which his mother lives:

"Death row inmates do not receive dental care, and she has lost most of her teeth. She is only allowed to leave her cell for exercise, a bath, or to go to the visitor's room. She exercises twice a week in a large enclosure that would be more suitable for dogs, and always alone. Likewise, baths are only permitted twice a week. My mother cannot talk to other inmates, and all her meals are served in her cell. The television is only allowed a few times a year, during consecutive public holidays. She cannot receive visits or even mail from people outside her family. If someone sends her a card, they inform her of its arrival, tell her who it's from, but she is not allowed to see it, let alone read it."

If Masumi is innocent, these conditions are indeed deplorable. But if she is guilty, most observers in Japan would say that this is a punishment well deserved.

As I write these lines, Masumi Hayashi is 62 years old. She has spent nearly fifteen years on death row, constantly fighting for her freedom.

There is a real culprit out there.
I'm determined to prove my
innocence.

In Japan, death row inmates are not informed in advance of their execution date, so neither Masumi nor the public knows when it will take place. Even if the sentence is carried out, it is uncertain. The accused could succumb to natural causes before that. Only time will tell if we will ever know the full truth about what happened during the 1998 matsuri in Sonobe. The "curry murders" will remain forever in the annals of Japanese criminal history as an incredibly sinister and horrifying case, and Masumi Hayashi, in the collective memory and until proven otherwise, is still considered the most evil woman in Japan.

RIE ISOGAI, VICTIM OF THE DARK WEB

Are you familiar with the dark web? You've probably never ventured there yourself with your mouse. It's the invisible part of the internet, accessible only through a specific browser called Tor, which is easily downloadable. There's no law prohibiting you from browsing the *dark* web and exploring the hidden, unofficial side of the internet.

It all depends on the places you visit, as most users frequent the dark web to engage in illegal activities: drug sales, firearms trafficking, trading in child exploitation material, buying and selling sensitive login credentials and passwords, counterfeiting money, lists of credit card numbers (with security codes, of course), and even hiring hackers. You can even find sites offering the services of hitmen! Hiring an assassin with just a few clicks, paid in cryptocurrency, with guaranteed service and confidentiality.

I've already covered several criminal cases on my YouTube channel involving people looking to hire hitmen to eliminate a family member or acquaintance. (Most of them end up committing the murder themselves and getting caught within 30 days, but that's another story. . .)

These are just some of the delights you can find on the dark web. The full list could easily fill every page of my book!

Since nothing is regulated there and no laws apply, most sites on the dark web are scams, and law enforcement agencies worldwide keep a close watch. You really need to know the right address to find "serious" people.

The dark web attracts thousands of scammers—but also future murderers.

On August 16, 2007, a certain Yamashita (a pseudonym, of course) posted a message on a forum:

"I just got out of prison. Would you like us to work together on something in the Tōkai region?"

This seemingly innocuous question, this offer of services, would mark the beginning of the Rie Isogai case, which, just a few days later, would end in bloodshed. Criminals and killers would join forces—and the outcome would be very, very grim.

A MEETING ON THE *DARK* WEB

First, let me tell you who is hiding behind the pseudonym Yamashita. This man's real name is Kenji Kawagishi, a 40-year-old in a rather dire situation—let me explain.

Kenji is unemployed and constantly in need of money. And working an honest job? That's not part of his philosophy. He lives in a van parked in Chikusa, one of the sixteen wards of Nagoya, a major city on Honshu Island, located 250 miles (400 km) southwest of Tokyo. Chikusa is a relatively affluent residential area. It's home to the city zoo, a pencil-shaped observation tower standing 440 feet (134 m) tall, and the prestigious Nagoya University.

Kenji, on the other hand, never went to university. He has always been an outsider. Now, he spends his days on the dark web. To be fair, he has suffered from a severe kidney disease since childhood, which made him physically weak and a target of ridicule and bullying at school.

Kenji made a lot of money through the dark web, buying bank account numbers and engaging in fraudulent transactions. His technique involved impersonating a bank employee, calling individuals and businesses, and convincing them to transfer money into an account he controlled.

He also employed the ore-ore sagi method (ore-ore means "it's me," and sagi means "scam"). This scheme targeted elderly and vulnerable people. He would call them and open the conversation with a loud "It's me!" After a moment of hesitation, the victim would usually mention a name, and Kenji would roll with it, pretending to be that person. He would then fabricate a story—car trouble, a robbery or temporary financial hardship—and plead for a bit of financial help. A simple bank transfer would suffice.

Unfortunately, Kenji had a spending problem, and nothing was ever enough for him. His greed led to his downfall. In 2005, he was caught, convicted, and sentenced to one year and two months in prison, with a four-year probation period.

In the process, Kenji lost his apartment because he could no longer repay his loan, and also his wife and four children, who left when Kenji, feeling cornered, began to abuse them.

To summarize: Kenji is a scammer, a fraudster, a violent husband and father, a ruined man. Quite the character. . .

Upon his release from prison, and after attempting to work temporary jobs for a few months, Kenji chose to further marginalize himself. To escape from his creditors, he decided to move into a van. No more fixed address. . . No more debt collectors knocking at his door almost daily.

But he still needed to live and make money. So Kenji had the brilliant idea of turning to an underground criminal job site that operates on the dark web: the Dark Employment Security Office, a kind of forum where small ads can be posted. It's exactly here that "Yamashita" writes his message. This time, he doesn't want to act alone. He is looking for accomplices to pull off a new scam. Two men quickly bite the virtual bait. They're Tsukasa Kanda, 36, and Yoshitomo Hori, 32.

Let me introduce you to their backgrounds. . .

Let's start with Tsukasa. He had a terrible childhood, abused by his father who would beat him severely, and he was also bullied at school. He suffers from a chronic illness: cluster headaches, also known as cluster migraines. These headaches are intense, localized around the eye, and typically radiate to the temple. Unlike tension headaches, they affect only one side of the head and occur cyclically, often at the same time and time of year. They are known to be extremely painful, more so than childbirth or kidney stones. Tsukasa has never been treated for this condition.

After graduating from high school, he decided to withdraw from society and worked for gangs. With them, he committed minor offenses before turning to the dark web to continue his criminal activities. In 2006, he was sentenced to three years of probation for fraud. He then tried to straighten out, finding a job as an assistant, but spent most of his time borrowing money from his girlfriend. When he responded to Kenji's ad, Tsukasa was in a desperate situation, seeking a way to make money while still staying on the fringes of society.

Yoshitomo has a different background compared to his two future accomplices. He doesn't have a criminal record and is new to the dark web. However, his past is no less troubled than theirs. Yoshitomo and his siblings grew up in a terrifying family environment. His father would beat the children violently and had numerous affairs, causing great conflicts in the parental relationship.

Yoshitomo had sworn to stay faithful to his wife, but eventually, he followed in his father's footsteps, ending up divorced and separated from his children. Due to his poor physical condition and, more significantly, his laziness, the youngest member of the future gang didn't want to work. He always managed to live with his girlfriends, from whom he would also extract large sums of money. When one caught on to his schemes, he would simply leave and always find a new one. A true cuckoo!

By 2007, when this case begins, Yoshitomo is deeply in debt. He has just been dumped again because he had been abusing his girlfriend's credit card. He wants to make money quickly and a lot of it to pay off his debts. That's when he connects to the Dark Employment Security Office, hoping to find a lucrative deal. He posts a message on the forum:"Are there any jobs available around Nagoya?"

Kenji responded to Yoshitomo's message in July, and the two agreed to meet up soon after to discuss ways to make easy money together and devise new scams. However, the meetings they scheduled kept getting canceled—one would cancel for a reason, then the other would follow suit with an excuse. They temporarily lost contact.

Kenji's new message on the forum in August reignites their mutual interest. Yoshitomo responds:

"To make a small fortune, we should kidnap people."

Tsukasa is hooked as well, and so is Yuichiro Hondo, a 29-year-old unemployed man. Their real-life meeting is about to happen. But the worst is yet to come.

THE FIRST CRIMES

The meeting between Kenji, Yoshimoto, and Yuichiro took place on August 21, 2007. Tsukasa, absent at this first meeting, was informed of the discussions later through an email.

What did the three criminals decide that day? They came up with the idea of robbing a wealthy pachinko player, who was also a former boss of Yoshimoto. And they wanted to act immediately. They spent very little time preparing for the robbery because they were so eager to get their hands on the money. They planned to carry out the heist that very evening, which may seem surprising, right? They weren't experts in robbery, far from it. And they didn't even bother to come up with a proper plan. They were going to do it "on the fly," just like that.

The three men did, however, think to equip themselves: rope, handcuffs, gloves and. . . a hammer. They needed a weapon in case things didn't go as planned. They jumped into Kenji's van and headed towards the workplace of their future victim in the center of Nagoya. Their plan was set: they would kidnap the man, steal his bank card, threaten to smash his head with a hammer if he didn't give them his PIN, and withdraw as much money as possible from an ATM. They waited for him to leave and get into his car. They followed him at a distance as the pachinko player headed home.

However, they followed him from too far away. Kenji, driving his junk car, lost track of him. When they discussed the failure with Tsukasa, he didn't just shrug it off. He arranged to meet the group at 10 p.m. that same evening at Kanayama station and told them that they needed to try the kidnapping again. This time, he would be involved. Stung by their earlier failure, Yuichiro returned home. He would not take part in the second attempt.

Pachinko

Pachinko is a device that combines elements of both pinball and slot machines. Players purchase a large number of small metal balls, which they then insert into the pachinko machine. The metal balls fall onto a vertical playing surface filled with numerous pins, sometimes bypassing them, but occasionally landing in certain holes that trigger a sort of jackpot with three spinning wheels. If three identical symbols align on a spin, the machine dispenses a large number of balls, which the player can either continue using to play or exchange at the prize counter for a gift or trinkets. The only control the player has is the speed at which the balls fall.

This ball-based system may seem unusual from a Western perspective. However, due to an article in the Japanese Penal Code of 1907, which remains unamended, gambling is prohibited by Japanese law. Since coins cannot be dispensed from the pachinko machine, but balls can, it provides a legal loophole.

Japanese individuals who violate this law face a fine of 500,000 yen (about $3,400); those repeatedly convicted of gambling offenses may face a prison sentence of three years. There are over five million pachinko machines, making it a very popular game in Japan.

On August 22, around 4 p.m., Kenji, Tsukasa, and Yoshitomo meet at the pachinko salon where their target is playing. They begin to follow him, and this time, they manage to track him to his home, a luxurious apartment in the Chikusa district. Once there, they face a new problem: the building where the man lives is very secure. There are surveillance cameras everywhere. They hesitate. Should they take the risk and break into the building, and then into

the apartment, knowing they might be filmed? No, definitely not. The building's security level is too high.

They leave the location and meet Yuichiro at the Tsutaya parking lot at 6 p.m. Tsukasa, who is very upset about having to postpone the kidnapping again, then says:

"At worst, we kill him. O.K. with you?"

While Kenji and Yoshitomo approve, Yuichiro is shaken. He doesn't want to commit murder. He had already had doubts about the robbery. In Japan, a murder could lead to a life sentence or even the death penalty. . .

This reaction dampens the enthusiasm of the other three. Being a criminal isn't as easy as it seems. There's a big difference between scamming people on the dark web, comfortably sitting at a computer, and actually taking action on the streets of Nagoya.

Tsukasa suggests to his new friends that they do some shopping to relax. He has managed to open a bank card under someone else's name and plans to use it for small purchases. Together, they manage to buy two packs of cigarettes and a gold necklace at a Don Quijote store. These kinds of petty thefts are more in their wheelhouse, and they're quite pleased with themselves. After the purchase of the necklace, however, the card stops working—likely because the issuer has flagged the scam. But it's not a total loss: they haven't completely wasted the day. They can still smoke, at the expense of their victim, in the parking lot while reflecting and discussing their future plans.

The four men abandon the idea of robbing the wealthy pachinko player. Too bad, he was supposed to have a lot of money in his account. But they need to start with smaller targets. One suggests kidnapping prostitutes—they don't have families, so they won't go to the police. However, the others disagree: a prostitute is not likely to be wealthy, and does she even have a bank account? Furthermore, they have pimps for protection, and these pimps are not exactly saints. Some of them are even connected to the Yakuza, the local mafia. So it's a very bad idea.

They can't agree. Tensions rise. Tsukasa and Yoshimoto leave the meeting. Yuichiro takes the opportunity to voice his strong dislike for Tsukasa, calling him too extreme, too dangerous, and above all, incompetent. He proposes excluding Tsukasa from the group. Things are already starting to fall apart, even though they have yet to achieve any success. This doesn't bode well for the future.

Kenji and Yuichiro, however, get along the best. They decide to plan a job together. This time, they will succeed, and it will be smooth, clean, and without any mistakes. Well, it's not going to be the heist of the century in Japan, but Kenji proposes breaking into the office of a plumber for whom he used to work. The man still keeps cash in his office. Deal.

At around midnight on August 24, in the small town of Nagakute, located in the suburbs of Nagoya, the criminals are at work. Yuichiro uses a screwdriver to break the window of the plumber's office entrance. They enter and start searching. But, strangely, they don't find a safe or even a single banknote. Nothing. Yuichiro becomes angry with Kenji and acts arrogantly. Kenji, in turn, gets upset. He leaves the scene, threatening to report his partner to the police.

Another failed attempt. Then, Yuichiro, full of doubt, acts in a very peculiar way. Terrified that Kenji might report him, he decides to take matters into his own hands. He enters a phone booth near the plumber's office, dials the police, and gives them a detailed account of the failed robbery. He is immediately arrested for attempted theft. It is 3:20 a.m.

Yuichiro is quickly tried and sentenced to two years in prison. During his official interrogation, he obviously mentions Kenji's presence during the burglary. He even explains that he met him via the dark web and the Dark Employment Security Office website. However, the four men had never shared their true identities, only using pseudonyms. As a result, the police are unable to trace Kenji.

Yuichiro is now out of the game. The trio involved in the Rie Isogai case, the one I introduced at the beginning of the story, is now complete.

Kenji, Tsukasa, and Yoshitomo arrange to meet on the afternoon of August 24 in a parking lot before treating themselves to dinner at a restaurant in Nagoya to come up with a new plan. They are eager to pull off a successful operation. Kenji, in particular, urgently needs money. If he doesn't find 300,000 yen (around $2,000) by the end of the week, he'll be in serious trouble. They need to act quickly and decisively this time.

The idea of kidnapping someone to steal their bank card and force them to reveal their PIN gains their favor. But Tsukasa insists—it's better to kill the victim afterward because, otherwise, they would go to the police, and the three would risk being hunted down.

Rich pachinko players? That's a bad idea. Too risky. No, what they need is a simple-looking office worker, someone who earns a decent living but isn't too extravagant so that their bank account is well-stocked. Between 20 and 30 years old, no children. Petite and frail, preferably—it would make it easier to kidnap her and toss her into the van.

This time, the three men are satisfied with themselves. They have a real plan, thought out to the smallest detail. Everything is ready, and they intend to act that very evening. So, they leave the restaurant around 8 p.m. and start driving through the streets of Nagoya in their van. Three hours pass without them finding a single victim matching their desired profile. Tsukasa grumbles.

Then, finally, around 11 p.m., as the van drives down a street in the Chikusa district, they spot a young woman, petite, with a sweet and smiling face. The rare bird they've been waiting for. The three accomplices are determined to cage her immediately.

This simple office worker's name is Rie Isogai. She is 31 years old. And she will never see 32.

RIE ISOGAI

Born on July 20, 1976, Rie Isogai lost her father to acute leukemia when she was just two years old. From then on, she was raised solely by her mother, Fumiko. As an only child of a single parent, Rie developed an incredibly strong bond with her mother, who did everything she could to provide the best possible childhood for her daughter. They have always adored each other, and that love has endured through the years.

Rie was described by her high school teachers as a "wonderful student." She left university relatively early—perhaps the only point of contention she ever had with her mother—to enter the workforce. She became a diligent and well-regarded office worker. Her goal was to save 100,000 yen per month (about $700) for a very specific and noble purpose. In her personal life, Rie was a caring and honest young woman.

At the age of 30, Rie began playing Go, a Chinese strategy game with rules dating back over 4,500 years, making it one of the oldest board games in the world. The rules are deceptively simple and can be learned quickly. The game pits two opponents against each other, who take turns placing black and white stones on the intersections of a grid-patterned board. The objective is to control the board by building "territories." Stones that are surrounded become "prisoners," and the winner is the player with the most territories and prisoners combined.

However, reaching a high level of play requires intellectual skill, strategic thinking, and subtlety in maneuvering the game. Patience is also essential, much like in chess. Go is a game that teaches discipline and an open mind.

You've likely seen this game before in a picture or a movie—a sort of board covered with small black and white stones. But if you haven't, it's not a big deal. It won't be important for the rest of this story, so don't worry. . .

Given her sharp intelligence, it's no surprise that Rie took an interest in Go, quickly becoming an avid player. This was especially true after she started engaging in intense matches against Taki Masato, an undergraduate mathematics student she met in April 2007 at a Go café. They connected so well over the game board that they ended up on another rectangular surface—a bed. Over the summer, their relationship grew even stronger. Rie would call Taki on her cell phone as soon as she left the office to talk about anything and everything. It reassured her to have her boyfriend on the line as she walked through the streets of Nagoya to her apartment in Jiyūgaoka (even though Japan has an extremely low violent crime rate and is ranked as one of the safest countries in the world).

On the evening of August 24, Taki wasn't home to answer her call. It was later than usual, 11 p.m. Rie had attended a farewell party for a coworker. Taki could have had the chance to hear his girlfriend's voice one last time. And perhaps, the three criminals watching her from behind the van's windows might have hesitated if Rie had been on the phone. . .

But sadly, for her, that wasn't the case.

RIE'S ORDEAL

The young woman is only about a hundred meters from her home when, suddenly, a man appears out of nowhere and asks her for directions. Before Rie has a chance to respond, the man forcefully covers her mouth with his hand. An engine roars, and a van pulls up beside them. Rie is roughly shoved inside.

In the back, Yoshimoto and Tsukasa gag and handcuff a completely terrified Rie. Kenji is at the wheel. He quickly leaves the kidnapping scene, driving the vehicle to the deserted parking lot of a restaurant located on the outskirts of Nagoya, near a national highway in a commercial district. There, no one will hear the young woman's cries for help or her heart-wrenching screams when they are forced to remove her gag so she can give them her bank card PIN.

Her small white handbag is ripped from her, and she is threatened with multiple knives. It contains cash (62,000 yen, around $425), which her attackers pocket immediately, as well as a bank card—the "prized possession" they had been hoping for.

Kenji is the most aggressive at this moment. He presses the tip of his knife to Rie's soft, pale throat, and as the young woman claims she can't remember her PIN under such pressure, he threatens, "You have five minutes to remember, or I'll stab you hard."

The five minutes pass, and Rie remains silent. What is the true reason for her silence? Is her mind so frozen that the code won't come back to her? Or is she keeping quiet so that her horrible attackers don't empty part of her account—money she has worked so hard to save over the years?

Tsukasa can't take it anymore. He orders Yoshimoto to stab the young woman in the chest. The man hesitates. His eyes are vacant at that moment. Should he obey the order?

It is then that Rie gasps out four digits, between breaths of panic: 2-9-6-0.

Tsukasa repeats the number to Kenji, who, to make sure he doesn't forget it, dials it into his phone before hanging up. Later, the police will find the four digits in the call history at precisely 12:45 a.m.

Relieved to have finally obtained the long-awaited key, and aware that they had achieved their first success, Tsukasa and Yoshimoto exit the van to smoke a cigarette in the parking lot.

Kenji stays behind with Rie, who begins to breathe a little easier. She is no longer threatened by the knives. However, it doesn't take long before she detects a new threat in the suddenly lecherous look of the Japanese man.

Kenji lifts the young woman's skirt and clumsily tries to remove her clothes. He asks for her help. Rie refuses, of course, and receives a pair of slaps. She starts screaming. Tsukasa and Yoshimoto throw away their cigarettes before taking the last puff and climb into the van. They grab Kenji, who, his face flushed, was preparing to undress himself to commit his rape, no matter what. His two accomplices don't hesitate to pin him to the ground. That's a no! The three men had agreed that none of them would try to sexually assault their victim. A promise is a promise, isn't it?

"Come on, Kenji. . . Calm down. . . We're about to succeed in our first operation. . . There will be others. . . And with all the money we'll extort from these poor women, you'll be able to pay for prostitutes. . ." Rie watches the altercation intently. Her ankles are not tied. She takes her chance and leaps out of the van. Outside, in the parking lot, she screams, but no one hears her. She starts running but stumbles.

Behind her, her attackers are already in pursuit. She won't get far. Back to her terrible prison of steel.

It is precisely at this moment that the criminal trio decides to eliminate Rie. So close to success, could they risk her escaping again? No.

They first try to strangle her with a rope, but Rie struggles, and none of the three manage to tighten it enough. Yoshimoto then fetches a hammer and strikes the young woman on the head three times. Bang. Bang. Bang. That should calm her down a bit, right? Blood doesn't just drip from Rie's head—it gushes out. Yoshimoto abruptly stops, even taking a step back.

Their victim still manages to scream. Then she starts groaning on the ground. Tsukasa grabs a roll of adhesive tape and wraps it tightly around Rie's head.

They wait. Kenji, jaw clenched, leans close to Rie, near her mouth, and notices through a small gap that she's still breathing.

So Tsukasa and Yoshimoto place a plastic bag over her head and, once again, a rope around her neck. This time, Yoshimoto pulls tight; it's easier now that their victim no longer has the strength to fight back. Meanwhile, Tsukasa picks up the hammer and strikes Rie's head forcefully more than ten times. You can never be too careful when you're so close to success.

2960! They finally have the card and the code!

The Go player no longer screams, no longer breathes. This time, she's dead.

After the trio smokes another cigarette in the parking lot, Kenji takes the wheel of the van. In the back, their loot—62,000 yen in cash—is divided into three. Fair enough.

The trio then stops to buy water from a vending machine in the neighboring town of Inazawa and proceeds to a Don Quijote store (a chain open 24/7) to treat themselves to clean new clothes.

At 3 a.m., the three men attempt their first cash withdrawal from an ATM. But they're unable to do so. In Japan, most ATMs are located inside banks, which means they have to wait for them to open to withdraw money. Realizing they need to wait until morning, Kenji, Tsukasa and Yoshimoto decide to spend the rest of the night getting rid of the evidence, starting, of course, with Rie's body.

At 4:40 a.m., the three killers find themselves in Gifu Prefecture, north of Nagoya. It's a mountainous region, lush and covered with dense forests. More specifically, they park their vehicle along a road in the steep forest of Kosato. There, they untie the body and throw it over a guardrail. The corpse tumbles down the mountainside for several seconds before vanishing into the dark vegetation.

Back in the van, Yoshimoto carefully wipes down the handcuffs, remembering he had touched them with his bare hands.

Back in Nagoya, the three men decide to split up. Kenji is tasked with making withdrawals using Rie's card. They agree to meet later in the day, after a few hours of sleep, to divide the loot.

At 9:10 a.m. in Nagoya and again at 10:35 a.m. in Chiryu, Kenji tries to withdraw money from ATMs. But each time, he receives the same error message: "Incorrect PIN." The criminal is furious. What? She gave them a fake code! That bitch. . . That bitch. . . So they went through all of this for barely $135 in cash each.

Later, because Kenji lacked the sense to realize it, it would be established that Rie didn't give them the code randomly—she did it intentionally to ensure her captors—and now her murderers—couldn't drain her bank account of its 8 million yen (about $55,000), which she had painstakingly saved to one day buy her mother a house as a token of gratitude for her unwavering devotion. She wanted it to be a surprise.

So. . . why 2-9-6-0? Well, because in Japanese, it can be read as ni-ku-mu-wa, which also means "I hate you." Rie, until her last breath, displayed an impressive strength of character that commands respect.

Kenji informs Tsukasa and Yoshimoto of the situation when he meets them in a parking lot. The others are disgusted. All they can do now is kidnap another woman. Not tonight, perhaps—they need time to process their disappointment. Tomorrow, yes.

Kenji then decides to take a nap in his van. The night had been long and grueling.

But he couldn't sleep. Something was bothering him. Suddenly, he was overwhelmed by immense remorse. The scenes replayed in his mind: the hammer blows, his attempted assault, Rie's body tumbling down the slopes of the Kosato forest. . .

On August 25, at 1:30 p.m., Kenji Kawagishi, against all expectations, picks up the receiver of a payphone and calls the police. When the person on the other end asks the reason for his call, he states word for word:

"I kidnapped a woman, stole her money, and buried her in Gifu Prefecture."

And so, the curtain falls on this short but intense association of criminals.

THE ARREST AND THE TRIAL

Less than an hour later, Kenji, who had provided his location to law enforcement, is apprehended by seven police officers dispatched from the Midori police station. Once at the station, the interrogation begins. It lasts only fifteen minutes. Kenji recounts the events coldly, from Rie's abduction to the moment he threw her body into the forest. At the end of this brief interrogation, the police ask the suspect to lead them to Gifu Prefecture, to the exact spot where Kenji and his accomplices disposed of the body.

Then, once they located the body, and only at that moment, the investigators decided to notify Fumiko, Rie's mother. When she received the call from an unknown number, she was on a golf course in Nagano. The police invited her to go as quickly as possible to the morgue at the Chikusa police station in Nagoya, where Rie's body had been taken. For Fumiko, understandably, it was a devastating blow. She arrived completely shattered and could only face the harsh reality: it was indeed her beloved daughter.

Later, she gave a heartbreaking account of that moment:

"When I touched my daughter's body, it felt as though she was still in pain. She had bruises all over her face, and her hair was disheveled, almost as if it had been glued together. Her body was covered with a blue sheet, leaving only her head and the upper part of her neck visible. Even looking at her like that, perfectly still, I couldn't grasp that she was gone. I asked my sister, who had joined me, what happened next. I have no memory of it. All I remember is wanting to hold her tightly, but I couldn't because I felt that doing so would hurt her with all those bruises. In the end, I remember leaning toward her and touching her cheek with mine, and she was colder than I ever could have imagined."

There was another harrowing moment for Fumiko later that day. The investigators, after corroborating Kenji's statements with the evidence, informed her that Rie had chosen to withhold her PIN, even at the cost of her life, to protect the savings intended to purchase a home for Fumiko. Upon hearing this, Fumiko broke down completely. Only the presence of her sister prevented her from falling apart entirely.

Following Kenji's confession, Tsukasa Kanda and Yoshimoto Hori were both arrested on the evening of August 25 as they were leaving their homes to meet and discuss a new kidnapping plan. After all, in their eyes, just because that fool Kenji had decided to turn himself in to the police didn't mean they should abandon their "business." Their arrest marked the end of their criminal endeavors. It didn't take long for them to also admit their involvement in Rie's abduction and murder. Their confessions always began the same way: "We met on the dark web with the firm intention of making money by kidnapping and robbing women. . ."

On September 14, 2007, Kenji, Tsukasa, and Yoshimoto were charged with corpse abandonment by the Nagoya District Prosecutor's Office. Barely a month later, on October 5, the case gained additional weight as evidence uncovered by the police led to further charges: abduction, confinement, robbery, and murder. Kenji was also charged with the attempted rape of Rie Isogai.

The evidence against the three men was overwhelming—starting with the meticulous examination of the van used in the abduction—leaving no doubt about their guilt. The primary focus of the trial would be to determine the appropriate sentence: life imprisonment or the death penalty.

Japan is one of the few democracies in the world that still enforces capital punishment, and it's generally reserved for cases involving multiple victims. However, the death penalty can also be sought in cases of a single murder if it involves extreme brutality or cruelty. This was precisely what Fumiko, Rie's mother, sought to establish during the trial. She vowed to dedicate herself to ensuring that the three men would be sentenced to death by hanging—the sole method of execution in Japan. This became her life's mission, a way to honor her daughter's memory.

Fumiko was especially concerned about Kenji's fate. His lawyer intended to argue that his decision to surrender and confess to the police warranted leniency from the court. To preempt this defense, Fumiko launched a national petition on December 25, 2008, calling for the death penalty for all three men responsible for her daughter's murder. Widely covered by the press, the petition gained significant attention. During a press conference, she made her stance clear:

"These are heartless demons. They have nothing human about them, and the only thing they deserve is death. I will do everything in my power to ensure that this sentence is handed down."

In addition to the petition, Fumiko created a website dedicated to her daughter. On this platform, she shared her thoughts daily about Rie, the perpetrators, and the upcoming trial. Her words resonated deeply with the Japanese public, with passages like this one leaving a lasting impact:

"Is it true that the weight of a precious life is less than the weight of the lives of these vile criminals? Who are we to judge the value of one life compared to another? Must two people be killed for the death penalty to be imposed? Isn't one life enough? To overcome this judicial obstacle, I have decided to create and submit a petition demanding the capital punishment for the murderers."

Within just ten days of the campaign's launch, the petition had garnered over 100,000 signatures. By October 23, 2007, Fumiko formally submitted the petition to the Nagoya District Prosecutor's Office, presenting over 150,000 signatures.

The trial began in 2008. Kenji, Tsukasa and Yoshimoto pleaded guilty to the murder of Rie Isogai, as well as the theft charges against them. However, each tried to shift the blame onto the others. An informal alliance seemed to form between Kenji and Yoshimoto, with both portraying Tsukasa as the ringleader—the mastermind who insisted that Rie had to be killed to prevent her from speaking. The two men claimed that until Tsukasa began striking Rie with the hammer, they had no intention of killing her.

Do you remember Yuichiro? The fourth man? The one who confessed before the group even encountered Rie? He also testified at the trial and pointed the finger at Tsukasa. Yuichiro argued that before Tsukasa's arrival, and before he assumed leadership of the group, murder had never been part of the plan. According to him, Tsukasa was the depraved individual, the psychopath of the group. Without his influence, their crimes would have remained small-time scams and petty frauds, with no bloodshed.

The prosecution, however, did not accept this narrative. While it was true that Tsukasa was the first to suggest killing Rie to silence her, both Kenji and Yoshimoto ultimately agreed and actively participated in the murder. They were just as guilty, the prosecution argued, regardless of who initially proposed the idea.

From that moment, the defense sprang into action. Rie's death had never been premeditated. . . It was murder, not assassination, the result of an escalation of events after the kidnapping. To appear tough in front of one another, the three accomplices invented false pasts as thugs and killers, each trying to outdo the others to gain respect and admiration. This led to a toxic rivalry, where everyone felt compelled to push the limits further and further.

Yoshimoto's lawyers painted him as a gentle, impressionable individual without true criminal tendencies. On the stand, the accused expressed deep remorse for his crime. The defense arguments were intense. Kenji's lawyer acknowledged that his client had initiated the entire affair by posting an ad on the dark web. However, wasn't he also the one who turned himself in? The only one, in fact, who felt remorse? Without him, without his confession, Rie's body might never have been found. His full cooperation with law enforcement from the very start deserved respect, didn't it? Clemency should be shown to Kenji.

By the time the defense made their closing arguments, Fumiko's petition had gathered more than 300,000 signatures. And the number continued to climb day by day, fueled by media reports of the trial. The prosecution leveraged this public sentiment in court, using both the overwhelming number of signatures and the national outcry to sway the tribunal. They even brought in the fathers of Tsukasa Kanda and Kenji Kawagishi, who admitted during the hearing that their sons deserved the death penalty.

Unsurprisingly, after all these powerful testimonies, the prosecution's closing argument demanded capital punishment for all three defendants with these words:

"The mother desperately desires a death sentence, but we believe this to be a natural feeling from a parent's perspective. It is our duty—and above all, the duty of the law—to honor her wishes."

On February 2, the defense responded, fragmented but united in their plea to avoid the death penalty at all costs:

"This was a one-time crime committed by a group of people who failed to communicate sufficiently among themselves. The method and specific location of the murder were not decided in advance. The killing was sudden. There was no detailed planning, and it cannot be considered particularly malicious compared to recent death penalty cases ruled on by the court. This is not the first time the dark web has been linked to a crime. . . Is that reason enough to condemn its perpetrators irrevocably?"

The verdict came on March 18, 2009. Yoshimoto Hori, Tsukasa Kanda, and Kenji Kawagishi were found guilty on all charges. However, despite the prosecution's demands, Fumiko's insistence, and the public outcry, only Tsukasa and Yoshimoto were sentenced to death. Kenji, because he had turned himself in, received a sentence of life imprisonment. The trial judge, Hiroko Kondo, explained the decision in the verdict:

"The court has determined that life imprisonment is an appropriate sentence for Kenji, who surrendered shortly after committing the crime. He contributed to resolving the case and, most importantly, prevented further crimes."

As expected, the two men sentenced to death immediately appealed their sentences. On April 13, 2011, the court, deeming Yoshimoto a sort of subcontractor in Rie Isogai's murder, reduced his sentence to life imprisonment. Only Tsukasa remained sentenced to death. On his lawyer's recommendation, he withdrew his appeal and was executed by hanging at Nagoya Detention Center on June 25, 2015.

Later, Yoshimoto was arrested again and sentenced to death for a double murder committed in June 1998, which resurfaced under curious circumstances. Yoshimoto was found guilty of the murder of Ichio Magoor, a 45-year-old pachinko parlor manager, and his wife, Satomi, who was 36 at the time. The crime took place in Hekinan, Aichi Prefecture. Today, he remains on death row, awaiting execution.

As for Fumiko Isogai, she continues to fight for the rights of victims' families. She has never accepted that all three of her daughter's killers were not hanged. However, she believes that Rie's death was not in vain. This horrific story raised awareness among many young women about staying vigilant and prompted authorities to closely monitor the dark web, a lawless space where deadly conspiracies unfold. As Fumiko says:

"I hope my daughter's death will never be forgotten and that it will serve as a warning to prevent similar tragedies in the future."

So, after learning about this harrowing case, do you still feel like venturing onto the dark web?

SADAMICHI HIRASAWA,
RUTHLESS ROBBER

THIS IS AN absolutely crazy story. It blends all the known genres that you're bound to enjoy, and it spans more than half a century. Truly extraordinary. But haven't I accustomed you to that?

This case begins like a great heist movie—a robbery carried out with an unprecedented and perfectly Machiavellian method. You'll quickly picture it in your mind, trust me, and those images might linger on your retina for a while. Then, we'll shift into pure crime drama territory, following the investigation of a completely insane thief who will give the Japanese police a serious run for their money. Next comes the trial phase—a courtroom saga unlike any other. And, in the ultimate twist, many years later, the story takes on the tone of a documentary, with tenacious characters refusing to back down. In the end, it's an unclassifiable case that questions Japanese society as a whole, and where it remains perpetually unclear whether the story has truly reached its conclusion—or not.

Dive with me into this historical account as we travel back several decades to the birth of what remains to this day one of Japan's most fascinating criminal mysteries.

THE MAN WITH THE BRIEFCASE

It is 1948, more precisely Monday, January 26. It's a gloomy winter day in Tokyo, with the sky heavy with gray clouds. The streets of the capital hum with their usual activity.

Japan emerged from the war barely more than two years ago. The population is still deeply scarred by the dropping of two nuclear bombs on the cities of Hiroshima and Nagasaki, which caused catastrophic destruction and the immediate deaths of 140,000 people (not counting those who would later succumb to radiation exposure).

Since its surrender (Emperor Hirohito had aligned with Hitler), Japan has been under American occupation. The economic situation is gradually improving. During the war, the Allied blockade had deprived the archipelago of many essential goods (including rice), leading to rationing and even famine in some regions.

Occupied Japan

After the signing of Japan's surrender documents on September 2, 1945, which brought World War II to an end, the Supreme Commander of the Allied Forces in the Pacific, General Douglas MacArthur, became the military governor of Japan. He earned the nickname "Viceroy of the Pacific." It was he who managed a war-torn, impoverished nation that needed to repatriate six million soldiers who had been deployed to fight in various theaters of war around the world. He also had to oversee the ceding of three-quarters of the territories Japan had conquered during its bloody expansionist policy in Asia from 1929 to 1945.

The American occupation forces, effectively governing the country alongside the British until free elections could be held, faced an appalling situation in Japan: poor harvests, cities in ruins, unemployment, a rampant black market, tens of thousands of orphans needing care, malnutrition, and a surge in prostitution. In short, the list of challenges was long, and it would take time for the country to heal its many wounds.

During this period, numerous progressive reforms were introduced, such as granting women the right to vote, ensuring freedom of the press, and abolishing imperial institutions like the Tokkō, the feared special state police.

On September 8, 1951, Japan signed the Treaty of San Francisco and a security treaty with the United States. April 28, 1952, marked the end of the American occupation.

Nevertheless, the United States retained tens of thousands of soldiers at its Japanese bases, as permitted by the security treaty. This remains the case to this day.

So, in 1948, the streets hum again. The Japanese are beginning to think that the end of the tunnel might not be too far off.

On January 26, 1948, a man caused the door of a branch of Teikoku Bank (also known as Teigin) in Shiinamachi, a rather quiet residential district located in the northwest of Tokyo, to creak open. The bank was about to close for the day, and the employees welcomed this smiling, impeccably dressed visitor. He wore an armband from the Ministry of Health on his coat and held a medium-sized black briefcase in his hand. He asked to speak with the director, and when the latter bent forward to greet him, he explained the purpose of his visit.

"I'm an epidemiologist with the Ministry of Health, but more importantly, I'm a health inspector," he said. "I'm on a mission ordered by the American occupation forces. There is currently an outbreak of dysentery, a form of diarrhea that causes the intestines to swell, in the Shiinamachi area, and it threatens to get out of control if we don't act now—quickly and forcefully."

This story seemed credible to the director and his employees. Given the health crises Japan had faced since the beginning of the war, the alarming words of this health inspector impressed the audience. Even more so, since he hadn't come just to raise the alarm, but also to bring a prophylactic treatment against the disease.

"This will help protect you against dysentery and prevent the first symptoms from appearing."

He then opened his briefcase in front of the astonished eyes of the gathered staff. He pulled out two bottles. The first was labeled "Medicine #1," and the second "Medicine #2." Some employees exchanged surprised glances. Were they all supposed to ingest these treatments right now? Who could say whether this was some kind of prank—or even a trap?

To dispel any doubts or fears, the health inspector places two drops of Medicine #1 on his own tongue and takes a generous gulp of Medicine #2. Well, fine. The bank employees are convinced and form a line to receive their dose. The epidemiologist administers a total of sixteen doses. The cleaning staff and their young children (who were almost impossible to leave with a babysitter at

that time) also receive the concoction. The liquids taste bitter, and the children hesitate to swallow it, but they have no choice but to comply. Confronted with the reluctant ones, the inspector remains calm, maintaining his friendly smile.

"If you won't do it for yourself, do it for others, so that the disease doesn't spread throughout the neighborhood and decimate it in a few days."

His speech has an effect; his steady voice does its job. Everyone takes the treatment. It's then that the first signs of discomfort begin. People start collapsing, one by one. When the first of them slides to the floor, groaning, a panic begins to spread—but it's already too late. In just a few minutes, twelve people lose their lives. The last four struggle against the toxic substance now coursing through their veins. They roll on the floor, desperately trying to hold on, refusing to succumb.

After one last glance at his victims, the health inspector, no longer wearing his kindly smile but now sporting a neutral, even cold expression, closes his briefcase. From now on, he cannot afford to waste a minute. He slips behind the counters and quickly, yet carefully, empties the cash registers. He collects a total of 160,000 yen, which at the time was equivalent to the annual salary of thirty bank employees (today, it would amount to only about $1,100). It's a nice sum. It's as if a human life is worth seventy-five bucks, a trifle. He places the money in his briefcase and exits the premises. The closing time has passed, and no one is likely to enter the bank at this hour. The fake health inspector disappears into the growing twilight, leaving behind death and despair in his wake.

Twelve victims. Ten died on the spot, and the last two passed away after being admitted to the hospital in critical condition. The bank's director, his deputy, employees, a little girl, and even customers, including a student who had come to withdraw money, were all victims of being in the wrong place at the wrong time.

When the news broke to the public through the press, it caused a true shockwave. The scenario was considered twisted, Machiavellian. The case immediately dominated the headlines of newspapers, and radio stations were filled with commentary on the matter.

A burning question then occupied the minds of everyone following the case: How could this fake health inspector have ingested the poison to prove his innocence to his future victims and not be affected by the substance himself?

The explanation is sure to surprise you. It took the investigators keen insight to uncover it. They owe much to the four survivors, who were interrogated at length afterward. Some had particularly vivid memories of the terrible event they had just experienced and were able to recall the assassin's actions in great detail. When he took his own dose, he left the pipette in the upper part of the liquid, while when he prepared the doses for his victims, he submerged the pipette to the bottom of the bottle, where a white, chalky substance had settled. This very simple action was actually the key to the mystery.

Hydrogen cyanide, which is probably the poison used, is an acid soluble in water. However, when mixed with agents such as acetone or ethyl alcohol, it causes the formation of whitish crystals at the bottom of the bottle—highly toxic crystals, a concentrated form of the poison. This chemical reaction effectively "cleans" the liquid in the upper part of the bottle. A man with this knowledge, and a particularly twisted mind, would know he could ingest the liquid in the upper part, as it would be only infinitesimally toxic.

Such expertise with poisons led the investigators to a trail that many would have preferred to never hear about again. It pointed to the infamous Unit 731, a military unit specializing in biological and chemical warfare. This secret laboratory had been shut down after the war, of course, but could it be that the man with the briefcase was a former employee of the lab? A chemist who decided to continue doing evil, no longer for his country, but for himself—and especially to make money? However, the Japanese police found no evidence linking the Teigin poisoning to Unit 731.

So, how could the investigation continue? The criminal seemed to have vanished into thin air. Yet, he left behind a clue that might have seemed trivial at first glance but would prove to be infinitely valuable to the investigators. . .

Unit 731

Unit 731 was a secret Japanese unit specialized in biological and chemical warfare during World War II. Located in the Pingfang district of Harbin, Manchuria (China), Unit 731 was not a typical military base. From 1937 to 1945, during the Second Sino-Japanese War and World War II, it served as the headquarters for all matters related to biological and chemical warfare.

Under the vigilant eye of Lieutenant General Shirō Ishii, the facility conducted a series of horrific experiments on living human beings. Many victims, primarily Chinese, were subjected to vivisections without anesthesia, deliberate infections with deadly diseases like bubonic plague, as well as a host of other horrific tests. Koreans, Mongols, Russians, and some Western prisoners of war were also subjected to these horrors.

Unit 731 also conducted experiments outside the laboratory. Evidence suggests that it was responsible for several epidemics in China while testing its biological weapons on unsuspecting populations in the field.

Yet, despite the scale and nature of the atrocities, many members of Unit 731 escaped post-war justice. In a controversial decision, the United States granted immunity to several key figures, including Lieutenant General Shirō Ishii, in exchange for the data collected from their experiments, which was subsequently exploited by the U.S. military.

THE INVESTIGATION

Did the murderer commit the perfect crime? Didn't he leave at least one piece of evidence in the bank that the police could exploit? In reality, yes. One single piece of evidence: a business card with the name Shigeru Matsui, an employee of the Ministry of Health and Welfare, who was regularly sent on missions to raise public awareness about various health risks. This, of course, is not the identity of the killer. He had received this card from Shigeru Matsui. It is a well-established tradition in Japan to exchange business cards when meeting someone.

To find the killer, Japanese investigators will therefore follow this lead. It won't be easy, as it turns out that Shigeru Matsui, who is contacted immediately, had distributed hundreds of business cards around him—593 to be exact. A monumental task begins, as you've probably guessed.

The Japanese investigators will attempt to track down, one by one, the people to whom Shigeru Matsui had given his business card. This task is made easier by the fact that Shigeru, a very conscientious government employee, kept a small notebook in which he wrote down the names of all the recipients of his cards. Even more specific, the business card found at the crime scene was of a particular type, especially in terms of the paper's weight. Shigeru had one hundred of these specific cards, of which eight remained in his possession. This narrows the list down to 92 suspects.

Thanks to the small notebook, the investigators will track down the owners of the business cards one by one, question them, and verify their alibis at the time of the crime. Most importantly, they are asked to show the business card. If they can, great, there's no need to go any further. "Thank you, sir, and we'll see you next time." However, if they cannot present the card—many admit to having thrown it away—the police begin further checks and will not leave the person alone until they are sure that he has a solid alibi.

Among these individuals, one man particularly intrigues the investigators: a certain Sadamichi Hirasawa. He no longer has the card in his possession and claims that his wallet was recently stolen,

PIECE A CONVICTION
EXHIBIT.B
N°120
BANQUIER
JAPONAISE

and that the card from Shigeru Matsui was inside. Well, why not? How can this be verified? He didn't report the theft? No, because what good would it have done? Well, Sadamichi, it could have helped prove your innocence... Too bad for you.

Moreover, when investigators search his home, they find a sum of money roughly equal to the amount stolen during the bank robbery—around $1,100. When questioned about this money, Sadamichi refuses to explain its source. That's a bad sign. Another bad sign: he has no alibi. At the precise time when the bank was robbed, he simply claims to have been wandering around the city. That's weak. Too weak.

Once Sadamichi is suspected by the investigators, things move very quickly. Two survivors of the massacre are called in to identify the poisoner from a composite sketch. And it doesn't take long... Both are certain: it's him. After hours of questioning, Sadamichi finally confesses to being the murderer. The police are elated! It's a miracle! The press is...

Very quickly, Sadamichi claims that his confession was obtained through torture. However, the police deny this, and at that moment, no one feels sympathy for the man who committed such heinous crimes. Sadamichi protests, insisting that his accusations must also be heard. But it's all in vain, and it won't be long before he is brought to trial. His trial is imminent.

SADAMICHI HIRASAWA, PAINTER

It might be time to pause and reflect on Hirasawa's personality. In a criminal case, it is always interesting to understand and analyze the psychology of the protagonists.

Who is Sadamichi Hirasawa? Are there any traits of his personality, elements of his past, that might lead us to believe he was capable of committing such a crime?

Judge for yourself...

Sadamichi Hirasawa was born on February 18, 1892. He was a tempera painter. Tempera (from the Latin temperare, meaning "to temper") is a painting technique based on an emulsion, either fatty or lean. To specify the nature of the emulsion, it's simply named according to its components: egg tempera, glue-based tempera, etc.

He was known and recognized for his numerous works and often participated in exhibitions throughout Japan. He had studied at the Japanese Institute of Watercolor Research, and after graduating, he helped establish the Japanese Watercolor Society. He was able to make a living from his art, thanks to exhibitions, which allowed him to find buyers, but like many artists, his income was not always consistent. A rumor suggests that during his lean periods, Sadamichi sold pornographic paintings on the black market. This could explain the cash found at his home if he wasn't truly the murderer.

Sadamichi married in 1916, and the couple quickly had two sons and three daughters. Well, it took a little time to conceive them, though. Otherwise, nothing particularly noteworthy about him. Clean criminal record. Oh, wait, one last small detail that might or might not be significant: it is known that Hirasawa received a rabies vaccine in 1925 because his dog contracted the disease. The vaccine caused severe side effects in him, and he began suffering from Korsakoff's syndrome, a neurodegenerative condition that leads to memory problems. The patient sometimes seems disoriented and has a strong tendency to confabulate, which means making statements and actions based on false memories of past events. Many believe this illness may have caused him to confess during his interrogation. He became self-convinced that he was indeed the killer.

But Hirasawa himself insists that he was coerced into confessing under torture. So, what should be made of his accusations? Still nothing?

THE TRIAL

The trial of Sadamichi Hirasawa began in 1950, just two years after the events. The country was still under occupation. From the beginning of the trial, the defendant retracted his confession, claiming that it was extracted under torture. The defense wanted this point to be heard, something that had been ignored until then.

The prosecution, on the other hand, continued to rely on Hirasawa's confession, with one additional argument. They claimed that potassium cyanide, the poison used in the killings, was only accessible to artists, as it was an ingredient necessary for their preparation of materials or colors. This argument was quickly dismissed by the defense, as the substance was actually widely available; it was notably used in the widespread suicides that took place in Japan after the war. This unfounded claim allowed the defense to counter-attack, arguing that the prosecution had poorly prepared for the trial. Furthermore, since Hirasawa had retracted his confession made under extreme duress, there were actually very few solid pieces of evidence.

Here is a list of the elements presented in the trial that led the police to arrest Hirasawa and bring him to court:

— His alibi is unverifiable. He claims to have been on a walk at the time of the crime.
— He is identified as the poisoner by several witnesses.
— He cannot produce the business card given by Matsui and claims to have lost it when a thug stole his wallet.
— A sum of money similar to that stolen from the bank is found in Hirasawa's possession, and he refuses to disclose its origin.

As the trial continues, support for Hirasawa's innocence grows, both nationally and internationally. His case becomes emblematic of broader concerns about potential miscarriages of justice, especially in cases based primarily on confessions.

Because, in reality, what formal evidence is there of his guilt? Can the prosecution produce material evidence linking him to the crime? Can a man be sentenced to death based solely on circumstantial evidence?

Despite the doubts surrounding his guilt, the trial concludes with Sadamichi Hirasawa being sentenced to death by the court in 1950. Until 1949, confessions were regarded as solid evidence, even if they were obtained through police torture. The Supreme Court of Japan upholds the sentence in 1955. Hirasawa's defense attorneys make eighteen attempts to have the sentence overturned by requesting a new trial over the subsequent years, but none of these requests succeed.

A JUDICIAL ERROR?

The question still arises, more than thirty-five years later. In the meantime, successive Japanese ministers of Justice never signed his death warrant, and thus the execution never took place.

In 1962, a Japanese writer, Tetsurō Morikawa, fought to save Sadamichi with the help of other influential people, such as the writer Seichō Matsumoto, lawyer Hiroshi Masaki, and critic Shunsuke Tsurumi. Even Minister Isaji Tanaka, who had announced to the press on October 13, 1967, that he had signed the execution of 23 prisoners on that same day, did not sign Hirasawa's execution, stating that he doubted his guilt.

On April 30, 1987, Amnesty International petitioned the Japanese government to release the 95-year-old man. Unfortunately, Hirasawa's health deteriorated, and he ultimately died of pneumonia in a medical detention center in the suburbs of Hachiōji on May 10 of the same year. But even after his death, the campaign continued. It was notably supported by Takehiko, Hirasawa's adopted son, who was completely convinced of his father's innocence.

In fact, there is new evidence pointing to Hirasawa's innocence. The composite sketch used to identify him by the two survivors was too vague and unclear to be considered reliable. Worse, the poison was assumed to be potassium cyanide during the trial. However, a contemporary investigation conducted by Keio University claims that the real poison was acetone cyanohydrin, a substance used by the military, which Hirasawa would have had no way of obtaining. It is also acknowledged that Hirasawa suffered from a mental illness, which may have impaired his judgment during the interrogation. On the third anniversary of the defendant's death, in 1989, Takehiko, his adopted son, presented new evidence to the Tokyo High Court in hopes of a posthumous retrial. The lawyers claim that he was wrongfully involved in the Teigin massacre and that he was the victim of a flawed judicial process. Takehiko presented strong evidence suggesting that the real mastermind behind the case could be linked to the chemical weapons projects of the infamous Unit 731 of the Kanto army. Documents from Bunjo Kai, a senior officer in the Tokyo Metropolitan Police who initially led the investigation, and twelve investigative reports supported this theory. Furthermore, documents uncovered by an American journalist suggest that the police ended their investigation into a former military officer due to external pressure, and this officer could very well be the assassin. The reason for halting the investigation? The man allegedly held evidence of an agreement between the United States and Japan: the absolution of Unit 731 members by the occupying forces in exchange for the unit's archives, which would later contribute to the chemical and biological research of the U.S. military.

To fully understand how Hirasawa was treated by the Ministry of Justice, one must understand the workings of the justice system in the archipelago.

Japan, on the surface, has an efficient law enforcement system, and its police forces enjoy strong public respect. This respect stems partly from their exceptional success in combating crime. Moreover, once an arrest occurs in Japan, the conviction rate is astonishingly high, with over 99% of cases resulting in a guilty verdict.

However, this efficiency raises concerns. There is a widespread belief that the police are infallible and make no mistakes during their arrests and investigations. This trust in the system is reinforced by the media, which frequently publishes the confessions of presumed criminals even before these confessions are presented in court.

Such practices have led to a deeply ingrained mentality in Japan where an arrested person is often considered "guilty until proven innocent," especially if they have had previous run-ins with the law or work in professions perceived as disreputable. In Japan, the burden of proof lies with the accused to prove their innocence.

Another notable difference from many Western legal systems is that the Japanese legal system does not employ juries. Cases are assessed solely by a panel of judges, a practice that most Japanese accept. Historically, there was an attempt to introduce juries before World War II, but it failed because many Japanese were uncomfortable with the idea of judging their peers. It's primarily a matter of mentality. There is also an additional fear among Japanese of negative societal reactions to their decisions, given the cultural emphasis on harmony and avoiding confrontation. As a jury member, one essentially has the power of life or death.

The emphasis placed by Japan on written evidence is another significant departure from Western legal practices. Confessions, once made, carry considerable weight, even if they are later retracted. While physical torture is rarer now, suspects are often subjected to prolonged detention and grueling interrogations. An accused person's reluctance to answer may be interpreted as a lack of remorse, which is an important factor in determining the sentence.

The story of Sadamichi Hirasawa highlights many concerns and criticisms that can be directed at the Japanese judicial system. A growing part of the public believes in his innocence, considering the delay in his execution as an indirect acknowledgment of a potential miscarriage of justice. However, Hirasawa's case is not isolated.

The case of Shigeko Fuji serves as another poignant example. Convicted of murder, she died in prison. Later, her family was able to secure a posthumous acquittal based on forced confessions.

The Shigeko Fuji Affair

In 1953, Shigeko Fuji was convicted of murdering her husband, Kamesaburo Saegusa, with a knife. She spent twenty-seven years in prison. During this long period, her daughter and younger sister fought with the justice system to have the case reopened. Initially sentenced to death, her sentence was commuted to life imprisonment, and the case was reopened in 1980. Unfortunately, Shigeko passed away in custody from cancer at the age of 69.

Six years after her death, she was finally acquitted on July 9, 1985, due to new evidence. Footprints found at the crime scene did not match hers, indicating that the true murderer was an intruder. Additionally, according to the second investigation, Shigeko had no motive to kill her husband, a claim she had consistently maintained throughout the trial.

All these cases highlight the need for deep introspection and reforms to evolve a system that prioritizes the prosecution over the defense. When the accused enters the courtroom in Japan, they are presumed guilty, and it is up to them to prove their innocence. The system certainly prioritizes conviction over justice.

The Hirasawa case became a subject of controversy and debate. About eighteen appeals were filed for a retrial and five requests for clemency. Despite this, each appeal was rejected, and repeatedly, successive Japanese ministers of justice were faced with the dilemma of whether or not to sign Hirasawa's execution order. Faced with this moral dilemma, no minister ever made the definitive decision to do so.

The Letter from Tetsurō Morikawa

Here s the letter from writer Tetsurō Morikawa, who defended Sadamichi Hirasawa, in which he strongly criticizes the Japanese judicial system. This powerful text, which draws on Japan's history, contributed to raising awareness among the citizens of the archipelago about their judicial system.

It is frightening to realize that everything, from investigations to judgments, is monopolized by people who live in narrow, sectarian circles focused on their own survival and professional advancement. Additionally, the power dynamic with the opposing lawyer, as well as the ideology and personality of the lawyer, are also deep issues. First, there is a contradiction in that the prosecution is funded by enormous sums of state money, while the defense must defend itself at its own expense. Moreover, the current judicial system makes no sense if the lawyers themselves fear the power and tend to conform to it. Recycle bureaucrats into democratic thinking, regulate arrests in separate cases, and rationally restore the jury system. During the investigation and analysis of this case, I became fully aware of the need for system reform, particularly the independence of the Human Rights Protection Bureau, the revision of the new trial system, and the total independence of the body deliberating on clemency.

The sentencing system must also be reformed. The abolition of the death penalty is necessary to prevent executions. We must also strive to improve the treatment of

everyone, from investigators to prison guards, to enhance their quality and strengthen their sense of mission. If these numerous intrinsic contradictions are not resolved, it will be impossible to eradicate the roots of judicial errors and false accusations. However, the most serious underlying cause of the illness lies in the way people think and their consciousness. Japanese democracy was not acquired through the awareness and resistance of the people. The Meiji Restoration was the work of the samurai class, and post-war democracy and the democratic constitution were created by the higher echelons of society, led by the United States. In other words, it was not born from the people themselves, nor did it naturally become the blood or flesh of the people, nor was it digested. Most people are now discovering deep in their bones the old ideas, consciousness, and customs inherited from the imperial system and nurtured during the totalitarian era.

People simply view prosecutors and judges, who are the same human beings, as sacred and believe they can never be wrong, and they unconsciously feel fear in front of prosecutors. This is also the reason why people sometimes provide complacent testimonies to them. In these conditions, the progression and speed of the disease of confinement vary by themselves. Unless we eliminate this tendency in the national consciousness to submit to power, the fabrications and false accusations of the authorities will continue. In short, this movement was a process in which self-aware individuals rose up and resisted a single judicial error committed by the authorities, establishing their own human rights in the consciousness of the people and acquiring a deep understanding of democracy. Its purpose is to foster growth. And to achieve this, the most important thing is to overcome one's own old thoughts and old consciousness. This is by no means limited to the problem of a trial or a judicial error, but extends to all the phenomena of the generation in which we live.

Some observers have taken the view that Sadamichi Hirasawa not being executed is already a victory. But that is not fair! Either this man was guilty and justice should have followed its course, or he was innocent, in which case a new trial should have taken place, and a new verdict of innocence should have emerged.

The painter, however, spent more than thirty-nine years in prison. . . before dying there.

Is the incredible case of Sadamichi Hirasawa over today? Not yet, as the lawyers of his adopted son continue to present new evidence in the hope of obtaining a new trial and the recognition of the painter's innocence.

In Japan, everyone will have their opinion on this crime, which made headlines during one of the most tumultuous periods in the island nation's history and continues to inspire writers and filmmakers.

So, was Sadamichi Hirasawa the man with the briefcase? He died in 1987, at the age of 95, in his cell, never having been executed, as if even the highest political and judicial authorities in the country doubted his guilt. The mystery surrounding the Teigin massacre remains, leaving Japan with more questions than answers. Guilty or not guilty?

And you? What is your opinion?

NATSUMI TSUJI, THE ELEVEN-YEAR-OLD MURDERER

Teaching is not the easiest profession. It has become a calling. In France, as in Japan, you are asked to impart knowledge to students who may not necessarily be motivated to receive it. Furthermore, the teacher increasingly plays the role of a social worker, managing students' family issues, bullying in the classroom or within the institution. And often, they do so with resources that are not necessarily up to the challenges. We've seen recently that one can even be killed simply for performing this noble profession. Yet, some still wonder about the lack of candidates and the loss of vocations. . .

However, let's not see everything in a negative light. When a teacher enters their classroom in the morning, they don't expect to experience horrific moments, a nightmare of a day, or for blood to be shed. . .

Yet, that's exactly what happened in June 2004, to a teacher at Okubo Elementary School in Sasebo. Sasebo is the second-largest city in Nagasaki Prefecture, in western Japan. A peaceful, residential city, home to a popular amusement park frequented by Japanese people, as well as one of the largest U.S. military bases. The large bridge crossing the Sasebo River that runs through the city is named Albuquerque, after a city in the state of New Mexico. The presence of the U.S. military has introduced several cultural elements, including culinary influences, into this part of Japan, such as hip-hop and hamburgers.

The horror occurred in a classroom, in what should be considered a sort of sanctuary of knowledge. The teacher enters. On the floor, one of her students, face down, throat slit. The victim was 12 years old. The murderer, 11.

Can this be attributed to an influence from the United States in this city, which is steeped in American culture? No. The torments of the human soul are the same in Columbine, Kazan, or Sasebo.

The terrible story I am about to tell you deeply moved and scandalized all of Japan and sparked endless debates within Japanese society.

So, come with me, if you dare, and open the doors of this elementary school. . .

NEVADA-TAN

Let's start by sketching a portrait of the murderer, Natsumi Tsuji. She was born on November 21, 1992, and was only 11 years old when she committed her crime. Due to her young age, Japanese law generally prohibits the public disclosure of her true identity. Why? There are multiple reasons. The first is that this child will one day become an adult. And when she has served the sentence society will impose on her, she will have the right to move on, the right to be forgotten. Condemning her entire existence. . . If there's genuine remorse behind it, if she understands and acknowledges her wrongdoing, and truly seeks to overcome it, to be forgiven, it is heavy, too heavy for a child. In the press, she was referred to as "Girl-A."

The Identity of Victims in Japan
In Japanese cases, the true identities of both the perpetrators and victims are often protected, which makes obtaining precise information about some cases quite complicated. Sometimes, entire articles refer to individuals as "Girl-A, Girl-B, Girl-C, Boy-E. . ." It's not easy for journalists or true crime bloggers, as well as for enthusiasts.

However, Natsumi didn't keep the name "Girl-A" for long. On forums and blogs, on the internet, she quickly became known as "Nevada-Tan." The reason? In one of the most widely circulated photos from the case, she is seen wearing a hoodie with the word "Nevada" on it. The addition of "-Tan" is common in Japan; it means "little"

in Japanese. There was also a slip-up when a presenter on the very popular Japanese TV channel Fuji showed some of the murderer's school drawings while accidentally mentioning her name, Natsumi Tsuji. This is how her true identity leaked. That left the choice of what to call her, and "Nevada-Tan" was chosen for conformity with the law.

Let's return to her childhood. There's no need to dwell too much on it. On the surface, the period leading up to her crime seems fairly normal. She was a very active child, balancing many activities. Nevada loved drawing and was passionate about the visual arts. She also enjoyed sports and played basketball on her school team. Nevada was a very intelligent young girl. During a psychometric test, she scored 140, which is enormous. Only 0.5% of the Japanese population has such a high IQ.

However, such sharp intelligence doesn't necessarily lead to academic success. Shortly before the tragedy, Nevada's school grades began to decline. Her mother then assumed that she was spending too much time playing basketball outside with her friends instead of studying. The mother imposed a coercive decision: she deprived Nevada of sports until her grades improved.

But this deprivation would drastically change Nevada's life. She had been a very active and outgoing child, and suddenly she became a girl who was locked in her room all day, which she could not stand. Moreover, her parents—especially her mother—constantly drilled into her that her high IQ meant she should have the best grades in school, and by far. She was only 11 years old! And they were already demanding that she perform at all costs. Japanese society is unforgiving in this regard, and this case is one of the most blatant examples.

So the child stayed in her room, and between her studies, she found a new hobby: watching cartoons on her computer, violent mangas, and horror films, which she easily found in abundance on the internet. At the age of 11. Her favorite movie: "*Battle Royale*," directed by Kinji Fukasaku, which was released in cinemas in 2000.

"Battle Royale": One Very Influential Film

"Battle Royale," the film, is an adaptation of a Japanese novel by Kōshun Takami, published in 1999 in Japan. Set in a dystopian Japan, the story revolves around a law passed by the government called "Battle Royale," designed to correct the behavior of the youth. Every year, a class is chosen at random and sent to a deserted island to kill each other under the watch of cameras. Only the last survivor can return home and resume their life with a certain sum of money. The idea is to offer the violence and entertainment that the youth crave for a few hours (yes, "Squid Game" and all the "Battle Royale"-inspired series stem from this 2000 film).

Some of the rules:

— The students are released into a restricted area that is constantly monitored by the military. Escape is impossible.

— The students are equipped with electronic collars that have a strong explosive charge. These collars are meant to keep participants in check and ensure they follow the rules. Waterproof and unbreakable, they explode if a student tries to remove them. They all explode if 24 hours pass without a single death.

— To win, any means are allowed.

— Loudspeakers are placed throughout the game zone, connected to the control center of the organizers. Every six hours, the organizers announce the latest deaths.

— The game ends when only one student is left alive.

— The winner is announced by "special flashes" live on television.

— The winner receives a letter from the president himself and a lifetime pension guaranteed by the state.

The film is extremely bloody and violent, regularly depicting murder scenes. In France, it is restricted to those over 16 years of age.

This film would literally fascinate Nevada, and she would develop a real obsession with it, watching it over and over. Her obsession quickly expands to include all things gore, films where blood flows. She becomes so consumed by it that she creates her own blog, where she shares disturbing gifs (animated images) showing graphic scenes and pure horror.

Nevada would also discover another passion, one that would quickly turn into an obsession: true crime investigation shows. She notices that in most cases, murders are committed with a blade, and a strange thought begins to develop in her twisted mind: Nevada would love to see how her classmates would react to the sight of a box cutter. One day, just before the summer holidays of 2004, she takes her theory into practice and brings a cutter to class. She pulls it out and shows it to others with a somewhat "hungry" look. Her teacher reacts quickly and confiscates it. Nevada is summoned to the principal's office. But, strangely, as you may notice, the incident is quickly dropped. No investigation is carried out, and nothing more is known. "Move along, there's nothing to see!" If only her parents had let her play basketball with her friends outside, right? Wouldn't you agree?

Nevada's fascination with this type of content began in 2004. At that time, Facebook was still in its early stages, and it hadn't yet revolutionized social relationships, while YouTube didn't even exist yet! Blogs were a new way to reveal one's personality on the internet.

Nevada talked about her site with those around her, and her school friends began to take an interest in what she was posting—this "forbidden" content that intrigued them. They left comments here and there. Most were supportive, encouraging Nevada to continue her regular posting of gore images and musings about a small part of her life.

However, Nevada quickly realized that not everyone was leaving kind comments. She became the target of bullying at times, with threats and hateful messages where she was insulted severely. Yes, even at the very beginning of the internet, anonymity gave many people the freedom to act out without consequence.

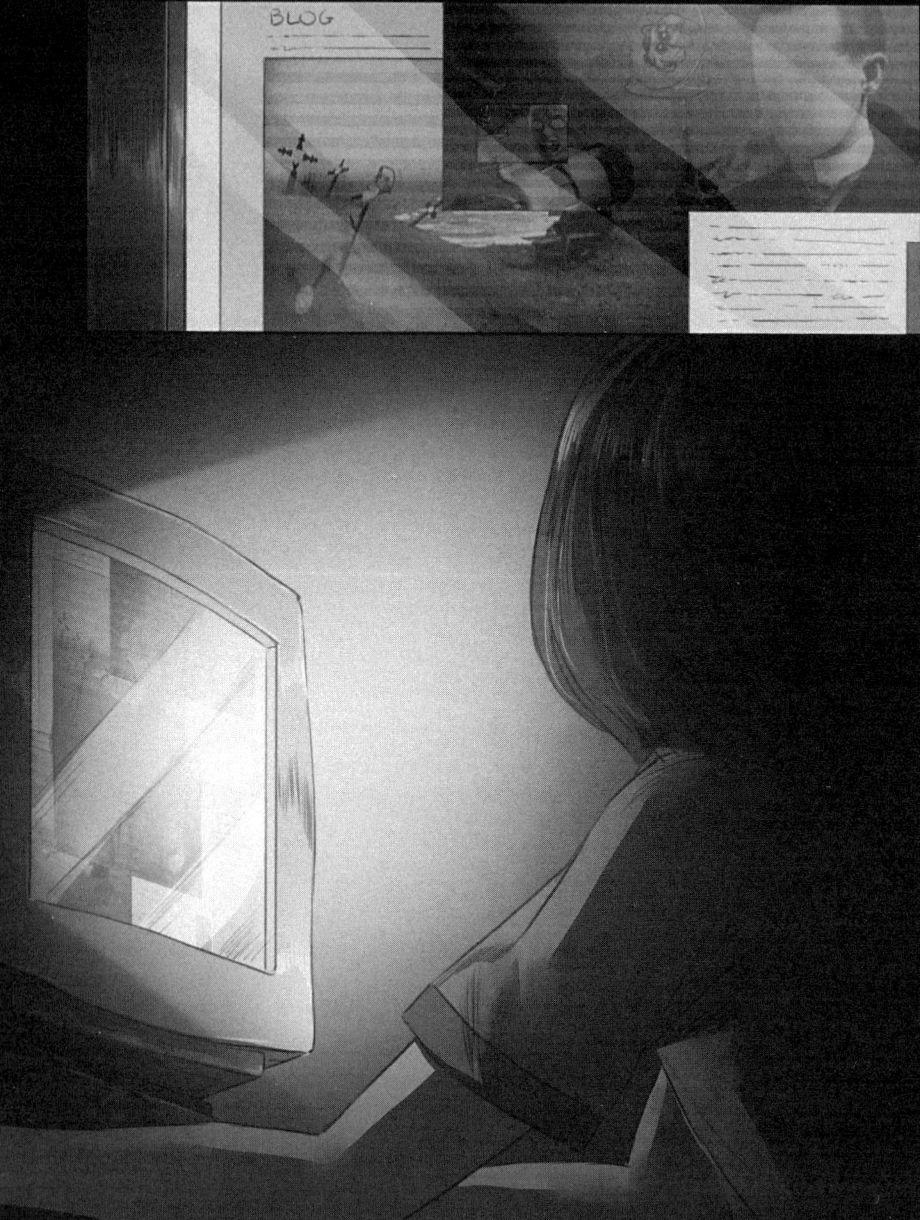
BLOG

A particular person consistently comments on Nevada's blog. This person is no ordinary commenter, as she is one of Nevada's closest friends: Satomi Mitarai. Satomi and Nevada are very close, almost like sisters. They are only about a year apart, are in the same class, play basketball together, and often chat online when they're not at school.

However, like in any friendship, there are also disputes and disagreements. One day, Satomi leaves an unflattering comment on Nevada's blog, calling her "fat" and "candy." Nevada demands an apology, but Satomi refuses to apologize.

Their friendship ends, which causes extreme aggressive tension in Nevada. At school, she starts insulting her classmates over trivial matters and spends even more time locked in her room at home, watching increasingly violent videos. It's as if, by losing Satomi, she also lost the lifeline that kept her from sinking deeper into the dark waters of her troubled thoughts.

Four days before the murder, Nevada receives another insulting comment from Satomi, once again mocking her weight. Other students also join in the bullying. It's clear now: Nevada is being harassed. Since she opened her blog, where she presented herself as "different" from the other students, she has received more hateful comments, endured far more criticism, and taken away little else but negativity.

The bullying, combined with her fascination with death and blood, creates a volatile and toxic mix that will drive Nevada to violence and the unthinkable.

School Bullying in Japan

Ijime (苛め/虐め), which could be translated as "bullying," is a term used in Japan to describe all forms of harassment, from simple mockery to physical aggression.

Bullying in Japan is a major societal issue. According to journalistic sources, it leads to more than 500 suicides annually among children and teenagers in the archipelago. This is a colossal number! It represents one of the highest suicide rates in the world in this age group. Authorities have initially attempted to respond by launching various initiatives to combat suicidal thoughts among students. The most surprising? One that involves printing anti-suicide messages or even images of cute kittens on used toilet paper rolls in schools.

It wasn't until 2013 that the Japanese Parliament passed an anti-bullying law, requiring schools to support students who are victims of Ijime. However, bullying is so deeply embedded in Japanese culture that it will take much more time and effort for the issue to be effectively addressed. Japanese society remains highly traditional, emphasizing conformity and social harmony above all else.

One of the most popular proverbs in Japan states: "The nail that sticks out gets hammered down."

THE MURDER OF SATOMI MITARAI

On Tuesday, June 1, 2004, Nevada and Satomi went to Okubo Elementary School in Sasebo like any other day. The morning proceeded as usual. At lunchtime, Nevada approached her friend Satomi, with whom she was currently not on good terms, and made an intriguing proposal. She offered to show Satomi a new and exciting game that she had discovered the rules for on the internet, if Satomi agreed to follow her into an empty classroom.

Once inside the classroom, Nevada immediately took charge, like a game leader. She guided her friend to a chair and took off Satomi's glasses, placing them nearby. Nevada then told Satomi to cover her eyes, but Satomi refused, so Nevada put her hand over her friend's eyes.

It was at that moment that Nevada calmly announced that Satomi was going to die. One might think such a statement would make anyone shiver. . . Worse! You and I would have jumped out of our seats, wouldn't we? But, surprisingly, Satomi did not seem disturbed. Perhaps she thought it was all part of the twisted game, considering Nevada's well-known obsession with horror. She likely believed that the game was about to take a terrifying and tragic turn.

In an eerie calm, without hesitation, Nevada took out a cutter from her pocket, positioned herself behind Satomi, and swiftly slit her throat. The victim slid to the floor. Large bubbles escaped from her open neck, along with a flow of blood. As a precaution, to ensure that Satomi would die, Nevada leaned over the body, which was convulsing, and slashed both of her wrists.

Then, she sat down and peacefully watched her friend bleed out before leaving the room. (This last image, perhaps the most horrific of all, was, however, not confirmed during the trial.)

Nevada wandered the school halls calmly, without encountering anyone, before returning to the classroom. She was covered in her friend's blood. At the end of the lunch break, when the bell rang to announce the start of the afternoon lessons, the young girl appeared in the doorway of her classroom, covered in blood.

Her teacher rushed to her, thinking that it was Nevada who was gravely injured. Nevada then said in a calm voice, "It's not my blood, Miss. I did something bad, you know." The teacher stepped through the door and found Satomi, face down, lying in a pool of blood. The young girl had already been dead for some time.

WHAT DO YOU DO WITH A PROBLEM LIKE NEVADA?

When the first police officers arrive at the scene, Nevada confesses to her crime, repeatedly saying, "I'm sorry." However, she refuses to say anything else. When asked why she wanted to kill her classmate, what her motivation was, she remains desperately silent.

The entire school is in shock when the police take Nevada to the local precinct to clarify the situation. However, it isn't until the following morning, Wednesday, June 2, that the young murderer agrees to speak.

Nevada opens up to the Japanese investigators. She explains that Satomi regularly humiliates her about her weight, leaves hateful comments on her blog, and that she had been planning her crime for several days. Yes, it's hard to believe, but not only does Nevada admit to the crime, she talks about her premeditation. She planned everything, at the age of 11. How she would lure Satomi into the empty classroom without making her panic, slit her throat to make sure it was over quickly, etc. She tells the police this, who are stunned and bewildered, as they take notes and record everything. Nevada speaks as if she's describing the script for a future gore film she wants to get produced.

Nevada also admits that, regarding the cutter, she had long hesitated. Initially, she had considered three methods of murder: the cutter, strangulation, or an ice pick. The ice pick—a nod to Basic Instinct (1992), an old classic, but one the young girl was familiar with.

While questioning her, the police also investigate Nevada's digital history, carefully examining the contents of her computer. It emerges that the schoolgirl harbors hatred toward many of her classmates. On one of her page's archived bulletin board entries, she wrote, "These are despicable and stupid people. I'm so tired of my class." Talking about a classmate, she commented, "So uptight, so ugly and so fat." On another occasion, she wrote, "Killing humans is unforgivable, and I won't do it. But I wrote some nonsense there. . ."

The police have the heavy task of informing Satomi's family of the tragic news. Satomi was the youngest child in a family of two brothers and one sister, who had lost their mother to a rapid cancer three years prior. Satomi's father was inconsolable. How could it have been otherwise? He lost his only daughter, his youngest child. In front of the press, he spoke of Satomi as a vital presence, one he could not live without. He recalled how his daughter had comforted him after the death of his wife. Despite her youth, she had been the most present and comforting, especially to the widowed father. Later, in an emotional and heart-wrenching letter to his deceased daughter, which was published in a national newspaper, he wrote:

"Why aren't you here? That's what I don't understand. Where are you? Have you already seen your mother? Where are you playing now?"

Since the age of criminal responsibility in Japan is 14, Nevada was not sent to prison after her interrogation.

Article 51 of Japan's Juvenile Law states that a person under 18 years old at the time of the crime must be punished. However, Article 8 of the same law, referred to as the Special Protective Measure, states that the age of criminal responsibility for a minor in Japan is 14 or older. This means that, technically, Nevada could have avoided any criminal prosecution for her crime and not even been sent to court.

However, due to the horrific circumstances of the incident and its widespread media coverage, which caused public opinion to strongly support the victim, the court decided to place Nevada in an institution. Given her age, her crime would not be judged in the usual criminal court. Specialized judges would determine her punishment. On September 15, 2004, just two weeks after her crime, she was placed in detention for two years in a specialized school for "dangerous children" in Tochigi Prefecture.

Minors in Detention in Japan

To begin with, let's define the term "minor." According to the law, a person is considered a minor if they are under 20 years old, which is the age of majority in Japan. However, a minor can be considered criminally responsible starting at the age of 14, depending on the case. Japanese criminal law classifies minors into three distinct categories:

— Minors aged 14 to 19: Criminally responsible.

— Minors under 14: Not criminally responsible but considered "minors deviating from the law." In this case, a child welfare center intervenes to manage the case. Administrative measures are taken to guide the minor back onto the right path, but they cannot be subject to prison due to their lack of criminal responsibility.

— The third category is more complicated. It refers to a "minor at risk of committing a crime." This term applies to young individuals who have not yet openly committed a crime but, due to behaviors deemed immoral (such as repeated running away, associating with places unsuitable for their age), are likely to commit one. They will be placed under surveillance and receive educational measures to guide them onto the right path.

Regarding the investigation of cases involving minors, the police are asked to avoid arresting suspects whenever possible. The public prosecutor has less authority than in France to detain the minor, and only a "family court" can rule on educational measures. Hearings are always held behind closed doors. If the minor presents an immediate flight risk based on their history, they can be placed in temporary detention for a maximum of ten days.

In terms of sentencing, Japan does not offer the same approach to juvenile offenders as many Western countries, including France. On the archipelago, the focus is on an educational approach, particularly supported by the "Juvenile Law," adopted in 1948, which aims to "form young people in a healthy manner." In essence, Japanese legislators prioritize the educational aspect over purely punitive measures. After all, what is the point of incarcerating a minor for ten years and then releasing them without providing the opportunity to reflect on the criminal act committed and without engaging in meaningful self-reflection while in detention?

Therefore, the Japanese justice system imposes community service on convicted minors to "repair" the harm done to society, as well as understanding programs to help them grasp the trauma experienced by their victims, stays to address drug addictions, and more. Each young person is assigned a specialized educator who supports them throughout their detention.

Since 2004, it is worth noting that juvenile delinquency has been on the decline in Japan.

Psychologists and psychiatrists were called in to assist and conducted a series of tests. At the end of this period, they concluded that Nevada suffered from Hikikomori syndrome. People with this condition isolate themselves and do not want to leave their homes or interact with others. It is also believed that she may have Asperger syndrome due to her communication issues and obsessive nature.

As a result of this diagnosis, Nevada was sentenced to an additional two years of imprisonment within the institution. She would therefore spend a total of four years there.

Murders Inspired by Books, Movies or Video Games?

At every mass shooting in the United States (and more broadly around the world, though most of these tragedies occur in the U.S.), the same question inevitably comes to the forefront, heard and read almost everywhere: "Is it the fault of video games? Was the shooter playing shooting games, those infamous FPS (first-person shooters)? Was he watching violent movies?"

The video game world and genre cinema are ideal scapegoats, a way to point to a culprit who isn't really to blame, rather than asking the right questions. And what about the free circulation of firearms in the United States? The possibility, in some states, to buy an assault rifle and keep it at home without the need for any permit? Since the late 1980s, all American politicians have agreed on the same topic when a shooting takes place: it's the fault of everything except the free circulation of firearms! Move along, nothing to see here. Or rather: look here instead of there.

It is hasty to make a violent work the trigger for a criminal act. Shouldn't we instead investigate the shooter's mental health, his medical history, his family background, and his social circle? Most of the worst criminal psychopaths had a terrible childhood, and in the vast majority, unhealthy relationships with their mother. Does that mean that everyone who had a difficult childhood. . .

Are individuals who have had terrible childhoods and poor relationships with their mothers doomed to become psychopaths or are they potential psychopaths? No, of course not. That shortcut cannot be made. Just as we cannot say that all players who engage in FPS games (such as Doom, Call of Duty, Counter-Strike, or more recently Apex Legends), on PC or console, are potential mass murderers.

Moreover, there is currently no solid evidence in any global scientific literature that establishes a direct link between violent media (war games, gory movies, etc.) and violent behavior.

Vanessa Lalo, a clinical psychologist and expert in digital behavior, explained this in November 2019 on France Culture:

"About 90% of young people today play video games. So, it is extremely difficult to make that argument. What we can show is that video games, with the competition they induce because you want to outdo the other person, want to kill them, be better than them, can create a certain level of aggression. But whether it's on Candy Crush, Mario Kart, or a first-person shooter game, the result is the same. Video games do not make people violent per se. On the contrary, since the 1990s, we've seen that with every release of a violent video game, there has been a decrease in crime, at least in the United States. The media can be violent, but it reflects society. If we buy violent games, it's also because our daily lives are violent. That doesn't mean we will develop associated psychiatric problems or that we will to take action. On the contrary, it also has a venting effect. And since we gain self-esteem by scoring points, feel better, and are connected with others, while our environment may not always be favorable, it may actually reduce aggressiveness or violence in individuals."

In summary, if political leaders truly want to reduce the number of mass killings, they should ask the right questions and focus on the real issues, rather than blaming their usual digital scapegoats.

Despite the detection of these two syndromes, neither of these diagnoses truly explains what could have driven her to kill her friend so violently. Many articles, citing numerous theories from psychiatrists and others, have attributed her crime and obsession with blood to the TV shows and films she consumed. Isn't that a shortcut? Many of us enjoy such programs, yet we don't develop murderous impulses or tendencies. . . So it's hard to explain these actions with just this simple hypothesis. Those of you who read my books or watch my HVF on YouTube, haven't necessarily become serial killers, right? I leave that judgment to you. . .

On March 18, 2005, Nevada and Satomi's classmates all completed their primary school studies. During the ceremony, Satomi's portrait was placed on an empty chair, surrounded by the other students. Her father came up on stage to receive the graduation certificate on behalf of his family. The scene moved many to tears. The students were also given an album as a graduation gift. Inside the album, there was an extra blank page where they were encouraged to add photos of themselves with Satomi.

At the same moment, within the walls of the Tochigi institution, Nevada also received her graduation certificate. This brings us back to what I wrote at the beginning of this story: this document is important for her potential reintegration into society and the continuation of her secondary education. It reminds her that there is a future opportunity to rejoin the educational system when the time is deemed appropriate by the justice system, which, let us remember, represents society and the citizens of the country.

On May 29, 2008, nearly four years to the day after the crime, the same judges declared that they would not request any additional sentence for Nevada-Tan and that from this point on, she would simply be placed under house arrest rather than kept in detention. Psychiatrists, appointed by the court, concluded after their various examinations that Nevada had developed the necessary qualities during her four years in the institution to reintegrate "peacefully" into society. However, they still recommended a probationary period, meaning she would be under house arrest. She could leave but had to return home every evening. In 2013, when she turned 20, Nevada regained her freedom of movement. She then moved with her family to an undisclosed location.

Nevada-Tan currently lives somewhere in Japan, her whereabouts are unknown, under a pseudonym. The journalists have played along and have never communicated about her since. We know nothing about her: her profession, family situation, etc. As I write these lines, the former schoolgirl is now in her thirties, and she may have even started a family. One thing is certain: since her crime and her release from the institution, she has never been heard from again, respecting the trust of the justice system that worked for her liberation, reintegration, and the respect for her anonymity.

THE CULT

The Satomi Mitarai case (also called the Nevada-Tan Case or the Sasebo Slashing) sparked an unsettling cult following online from the very beginning, with individuals portraying Nevada as a kind of psychopathic heroine.

Some of her self-proclaimed "disciples" even went as far as finding her former address in Sasebo and organizing pilgrimages to it, in a disturbingly twisted way, to honor her. A German rock band adopted the name "Nevada-Tan," while another band, Fecal Matter Discorporated, dedicated an album to her, featuring the chilling inscription: "To her and all the little Japanese girls who kill people."

Even worse, because it reached a larger, anonymous public, the University of Nevada, contacted by Japanese journalists, confirmed that in the months following the murder, the grey sweatshirt worn by the murderer in her school photo became one of the best-selling items in their online store. However, after realizing the disturbing trend and its implications, the university decided to temporarily remove the hoodie from its catalog to discourage inappropriate cosplay and the misuse of the garment.

This crime also triggered a debate in Japan about lowering the age at which a child can face harsher punishments from 14 to 11. A previous reduction of the age limit, from 16 to 14, had already taken

place in 2000 after the Kobe child murders in 1997. However, the new debate did not gain widespread support, and no political decision was made on the matter by the legislative body.

The Kobe Tragedy of 1997

The 1997 Kobe child murders refer to a series of killings committed by Seito Sakakibara, who was 14 years old at the time of the crimes. As I have shared in my YouTube channel, on March 16, 1997, he killed 10-year-old Ayaka Yamashita by smashing her skull, then stabbed a second victim, a 9-year-old, during his escape. Two months later, he attacked 11-year-old Jun Hase, strangling him before leaving his decapitated head in front of the gate of Tainhohata Elementary School.

At the time, the Minister of Education expressed being "deeply shocked" by the fact that the murders were committed by a high school student and promised an investigation into how much the educational system itself might have contributed to the tragedy.

A sociologist from the University of Tokyo, Professor Shinji Miyada, commented on the incident: "More and more children are rebelling against certain aspects of the Japanese education system: the wearing of uniforms, mandatory group activities, etc. This raises questions about the teaching methods for 14-15-year-olds. A reflection needs to take place with teachers on the revolt of high school students against the system."

Nevada-Tan will therefore never have truly explained the motive behind her crime. But does a clear motive even exist? Was it the culmination of the bullying she suffered? Her intense consumption of violent content? A mix of both? Or something entirely different?

In any case, this tragedy captivated the Japanese archipelago for many months, and there are few Japanese people of the right age who do not remember the horrific story of young Satomi Mitarai.

As for the cult that followed...

In conclusion, could one write that criminal history is an eternal recurrence and that, rather than deterring future murderers, past crimes give rise to those that follow?

THE BLOODY AWAKENING OF SAWAKO WATANABE

SHE IS A petite young woman with a delicate face, perfect eyebrows, and a carefully styled lock of hair on her forehead. She smiles in every photo we have of her. Sawako gazes into the lens with her beautiful black eyes. It's clear that she enjoys posing, she likes to please, and she enjoys being the center of attention.

One could imagine her straight out of a shōjo, those manga for teenagers with cute heroines who hide powerful abilities within them.

Sawako Watanabe, one of the two heroines of our story, is about to cross paths with another young woman who could also belong in a shōjo. But this one hides a macabre power: the power of death and destruction. And, as you might guess, she will express it in the worst way possible, otherwise, this case wouldn't be in the pages of my third collection.

The tragedy takes place in Osaka, the third most populated city in Japan. A vibrant, ever-moving metropolis that attracts young Japanese people with its unceasing dynamism. At first, it's the typical story of a young provincial girl arriving in the big city with all the financial difficulties that come with it. And then it spirals, not by force of circumstance, but by the twisting of a mind one could never have imagined to be so insidious and cunning. A sort of sitcom for young adults that turns into a horror movie.

So, let yourself be drawn into this story, which could just as easily serve as the script for a very gory manga. This is the horrific case of Sawako Watanabe. And it starts now, for you. . .

THE MEETING

Sawako Watanabe was born in 1993 in the Ehime Prefecture. She spent her entire childhood and adolescence there. Ehime is a rural city located on the small island of Shikoku, the smallest of the four main islands that make up Japan, far from Tokyo, the capital. It boasts breathtaking beauty that has inspired many artists.

In Ehime, you'll find picturesque bridges connecting small pieces of land, where one can enjoy cycling, but it's also a hiker's paradise, with mountains and two castles that still have intact original keep towers. Additionally, it's one of the four prefectures in the Shikoku Pilgrimage, a large loop connecting 88 temples and the Dōgo Onsen, Japan's oldest hot spring, which has been attracting residents, tourists, and pilgrims for over three thousand years. It's a very lovely destination for adventurers, for sure. However, when you grow up as a teenager in the Ehime region, the overwhelming desire is often to leave and head to a big city to live a completely different life and take advantage of the allure of a sprawling metropolis.

Sawako spent her entire adolescence with one dream in mind: to follow in her kind father's footsteps and open a flower shop. That is the only information she's willing to share with us. However, before taking over her father's vocation, she decides, in 2015, at 24 years old, to pack her bags and move to Osaka for a while. She wants to spread her wings and experience the life of a bustling metropolis, try to thrive in it. In short, she wants to completely change her environment and existence.

Where is Osaka located? It's about five hours east by road, so it's not at the end of the archipelago. It's an industrious city, one of Japan's largest ports, with a population of about two and a half million people. It's also a tourist city known for its many restaurants and attractions, such as the Umeda Sky Tower, Dotonbori, the famous Nintendo World Park, and Osaka Castle, a historical gem of Japan.

There's a unique atmosphere in Osaka. It's a city that never sleeps, where, at any hour, you can eat, dance, watch a movie, or see a show. The local specialties include okonomiyaki (a thick pancake made of flour, eggs, and cabbage, usually topped with a thick sauce, dried seaweed, and slices of pork) and takoyaki (dough balls filled with pieces of octopus, cooked in a waffle-like mold). Is that making you hungry? Feel free to grab a bite right now before continuing with the rest of the story, that's my advice as a friend...

To conclude about the location of the tragedy, Osaka is considered a bit of an anomaly. The residents are known to be sometimes more direct than in other regions of Japan, but they are also more welcoming and sociable.

The flip side of these many advantages is that rent for a simple place in Osaka is extremely expensive. Most young people choose to live in shared accommodations, with two, three, or even four roommates, depending on the neighborhood. Sawako, of course, is no exception to this rule.

In addition to studying, she gets a part-time job that barely covers her expenses, her food, and the rare moments of leisure. To avoid weighing down her unavoidable costs, Sawako finds a solution for her housing situation. She decides not to rent an apartment or a room in an apartment, but instead opts for the solution of *sharehouses*.

Sharehouses

Sharehouses are residences where it's possible to have your own room and enjoy shared spaces with other tenants. It is actually quite popular to use these spaces to socialize and interact with others.

The common areas in sharehouses typically include a living room, kitchen, bathroom, and showers. Some sharehouses even offer a community project, where residents share a common interest, like cycling or gardening, and organize events throughout the year to ensure cohesion among the residents.

These sharehouses are much more affordable compared to renting an apartment, even when shared. This makes them an attractive option for young people trying to manage the high living costs in cities like Osaka.

Sawako sees this as a great opportunity to make friends, save money, and ultimately feel more at home in this vast city by sharing her life with others. By choosing this mode of residence, she knows she will never feel alone.

And indeed, a new resident moves into the sharehouse in August. Her name is Terumi Morishima. Sawako takes her under her wing to explain the community dynamics of the place. Although Terumi grew up in the Osaka prefecture, her family moved to Hiroshima when she was still in elementary school. She lived there with her mother, stepfather, and two younger brothers until she finished high school.

Terumi hides a terrible secret. She suffered physical and sexual abuse throughout her childhood at the hands of her stepfather. To begin with, Terumi's mother was verbally and sometimes physically abused by her partner. Then the infamous character attacked the girl. The blows rained, then the man began to sexually abuse Terumi. The young girl hid it from her mother for a long time, for fear of upsetting her too much, but also for fear of reprisals from the rapist, obviously. Terumi ends up getting pregnant by her stepfather during her first year in high school. She tells him about it and he, furious, orders her to have an abortion. However, the legal deadline has passed and it is therefore without the knowledge of her own mother that Terumi gives birth at home. The child does not survive the birth and it is the father-in-law who authoritatively seizes the baby's body and throws it behind a dike, into the sea, so that no one will ever know about this dark story. Terumi says nothing about this tragedy to her mother, as she later conceals the death of her dog, the only companion in whom she fully trusts. She hides the remains and prefers to say that he has disappeared, for fear, again, of upsetting her mother. When Terumi is unhappy, she hides it all the time. She doesn't let anything show to anyone. To start in life, there are less dark scenarios than Terumi's, don't you think?

Let's return to the shared house in Osaka. In the shared residence, Terumi gets along fairly well with the other residents. Well, it's a little more than just "hello, goodbye." The truth is, the young woman struggles to find a stable job and lives off very short-term temporary work. Her income is often insufficient to live in Osaka, even within a shared house. Terumi spends much of her time locked in her room, on the internet, trying to offer her illustration skills to newspapers, publishing houses, or private individuals who might need illustrations for cards or stories. This would provide her with supplementary income. Unfortunately, her efforts remain fruitless, and the few clients she manages to convince always leave her financially precarious.

"She stayed almost all the time in her room, and I didn't see her much," one of her housemates would later state during the trial.

Terumi also seemed to be an internet addict, spending her whole day on her computer.

However, she enjoys Sawako's company, as she is the only one allowed in her space. The two young women form a friendship. But what Sawako doesn't know is that this friendship, at least on Terumi's part, is entirely fake. It could have been pure. . . but when money is involved, it often turns into disaster. Money and sex, the two most common reasons behind murderous impulses. . . There aren't many others, truly.

Indeed, Terumi immediately sees that Sawako could be a beautiful pigeon. She carries no visible trauma on her face and comes from a simple, relatively affluent family. So, she starts by stealing her identity.

Terumi grabs Sawako's driver's license and uses this document to approach several banks for loans. She disguises herself as Sawako, going from one counter to another, pocketing over 2.2 million yen, or roughly $15,000. She also opens an account in her "friend's" name, which is immediately overdrawn by 610,000 yen, or about $4,200.

Terumi would later explain, "I did this with outstanding professionalism and didn't expect to be discovered, really. To look like Sawako, I swapped my glasses for contact lenses, wore makeup like her, and applied false eyelashes. It really worked, and I managed to fool all the bank employees; no one doubted me at all!"

Just a few months after moving in, at the beginning of November, Terumi, enriched by the dishonestly acquired funds, decides

to move into an apartment located just a little over a half mile (900 m) away from the shared house. Why? Because the shared residence doesn't allow pets, and Terumi wants to adopt a dog again. She prefers the company of animals, which she considers superior to that of people.

Renting an apartment in Japan can be quite costly, often requiring up to six months' rent in advance, along with additional fees and deposits. But Terumi didn't make the mistake of spending all the money she unlawfully acquired under Sawako's identity on frivolities. However, after paying for the rent and the dog's purchase and upkeep, not much remains. Most of all, Terumi harbors a significant fear: the possibility that the banks might try to contact Sawako, informing her that the overdraft needs to be paid and the loan repayments covered.

This dilemma weighs heavily on Terumi, because if the financial institutions manage to locate Sawako, she will discover the scam, and everything could collapse for the forger. That's unthinkable. So, a plan begins to form in Terumi's mind. Isn't this the perfect time to make Sawako disappear?

After all, if Sawako believes they are friends, that sentiment is not reciprocated at all. . .

A SORDID PLAN

Even after moving into her new apartment, Terumi continues to frequent the sharehouse and has even stored some of her belongings in Sawako's closet. Worried, yet happy to finally have her own place, Terumi suggests hosting a Christmas Eve party in her new apartment and invites all the housemates, including Sawako, of course.

On the afternoon of December 24, Terumi asks her "friend" to help her with the shopping to prepare for the upcoming celebration. It's around 7 p.m. when the two women return from their errands, arms full of groceries. Surveillance footage taken from outside Terumi's building confirms this. It's also at this moment that Sawako receives a message on the LINE app (a Japanese version of WhatsApp) from a housemate asking if everything is ready. In response, Sawako writes, “I'm at Terumi's. It will take a little longer than expected.”

Just 15 minutes later, Terumi arrives alone at the sharehouse, claiming that Sawako is busy in the kitchen. Everything is fine. She leaves again and informs the guests that they will be notified by message when the festivities will begin. But after some time, when everyone begins to grow impatient, the housemate using LINE receives the following message: “I apologize for missing the party, but I have an urgent issue to attend to. Have fun without me.” It's signed by Sawako. But was it really she who wrote it?

Terumi returns to the sharehouse and bluntly declares that Sawako has disappeared. She left the apartment without a word. “Maybe she went to meet her ex-boyfriend, with whom she is still in contact?” Terumi suggests. Is that a possibility? Could that have been the urgent problem?

On December 25, Sawako was supposed to be with her parents in the Ehime prefecture to celebrate Christmas.

But she doesn't show up. She is completely unreachable. In a state of deep concern, Sawako's father reports her disappearance to the police on the evening of December 25, both in his city of residence and at the police station responsible for the area where the sharehouse is located.

Sawako is an adult. Generally speaking (and we've seen this in other cases in this collection), the police aren't obligated to act immediately or open an investigation. An adult has the right to leave or disappear at will. It's not mandatory, and the decision is left to the discretion of the officers. However, a few days later, in Osaka, an inspector decides to visit the sharehouse. Perhaps moved by the Christmas spirit, and also touched by a father's distress. It's surprising because, at the same time, Sawako's bank informs the authorities that her bank card was used at an ATM in Osaka. So she must still be alive. Or is she?

After speaking with Sawako's housemates, the inspector decides to visit Terumi's apartment, as she was the last person to see Sawako alive. This act of diligence proves to be fruitful.

When the police arrive on December 29, at 1:00 a.m., at Terumi's apartment, they make a gruesome discovery: they find a human skull and other bones in the bathroom, as well as human remains in the freezer. The remains of poor Sawako Watanabe.

Terumi Morishima is immediately arrested and charged with murder, desecration, and improper disposal of a corpse. According to an article in the Sankei Shimbun, a famous Japanese newspaper, dated the same day, when confronted with the evidence, the young woman allegedly said to the police, "Yes, there is a skull in my room, but I have no comment on that."

That's laconic. The discovery of the remains in the freezer is one thing, but a skull. . . That's worse than finding a severed head. A skull implies that the skin, hair, eyes, and all tissues have been removed. It's chilling. Absolutely chilling. It begs for an explanation, don't you think?

So, pressed by the investigators, interrogated relentlessly, Terumi eventually provides one: O.K., she found Sawako dead when she returned to the sharehouse on the evening of December 24. A heart attack, she thinks. She panicked and chose to say nothing, opting instead to conceal the body. She claims to have spent the next three days inside her apartment, mutilating and dismembering Sawako's body to dispose of it in the best possible way, because she was terrified, thinking the authorities would accuse her of murder.

But the autopsy of the lungs is clear: Sawako was suffocated on December 24, after 7:50 p.m. Another damning piece of evidence for Terumi: traces of a powerful sedative were found in Sawako's blood. A sedative that had been prescribed to Terumi to help her sleep. This wasn't a heart attack; it wasn't a natural death, Terumi. . . So what do you have to say about that?

No, she still doesn't confess. So the investigation continues, and more incriminating evidence keeps coming to light. . .

This isn't even a murder, it's an assassination—premeditated. Analysis of Terumi's search history reveals some rather odd queries if she were innocent. Judge for yourself:

— *How to dismember a human?*
— *Can bones be broken?*
— *How to stun a person?*
— *How to kill someone and commit the perfect crime?*
— *What happens to your bank account if you disappear?*
— *What happens if you take a lot of sleeping pills?*
— *Do you still deny it, Terumi, or do you speak up?*

She remains silent! A detour through the bank where the victim's card was used: 100,000 yen (about $700) was withdrawn on December 25, the day after the murder (Merry Christmas, Sawako). The ATM footage is analyzed by the police, and of course, it's not Sawako making the withdrawal; it's Terumi. They can't be mistaken. This means that before killing her, before dismembering her, her "friend" had made Sawako reveal her PIN. And what did she do with that hard-earned money, Terumi? You can guess, can't you? She goes to a big store and buys a freezer, a knife, a saw, a cutting board, trash bags and. . . a pressure cooker. It's Christmas, after all; she might as well treat herself to some gifts. . . But no, you'll see. . .

So, Terumi, are you going to confess now? Yes. It's time.

At this point, Terumi, overwhelmed, finally confesses everything. She recounts in detail the horrifying events of those three days.

She suffocated Sawako before dismembering her between the kitchen and the bathroom, using a knife and a saw. Sawako's hands and feet were cut off, placed in nylon bags, then wrapped in paper bags, which the criminal scattered around: the first half was stored in a closet in Terumi's former room on the second floor of the sharehouse, and the second half in the freezer of her apartment, along with other pieces of flesh, which were left in the communal house's kitchen trash. The idea was to scatter the body parts so that they would never be found, like a puzzle. Terumi disposed of some organs and bones directly in the trash bins of her building, throwing them into large garbage bags.

And what about the skull? As well as the dismembered spine and pelvis? Terumi cooked them in her new pressure cooker. Yes, you read that right. For fifteen minutes or more... Just like cooking artichokes... That's why the flesh detached easily from the bones. That's why the police found a skull...

After being broken down in the trash, the meat and muscles were placed outside the apartment with the other garbage. The pressure cooker was used to boil certain parts of Sawako. That's why the police discovered the skull, spine, and pelvis of the young woman submerged in a strange, dark liquid at the bottom of Terumi's bathtub. It's the kind of investigation that leaves its mark. It changes an inspector or detective forever.

All of this surely deserves a trial, doesn't it?

TRIAL TIME

The trial began in June 2016, less than six months after the murder, at the Osaka District Court. Terumi is accused of killing Sawako Watanabe and dismembering her body. The prosecution's case is strong. The defense will have a difficult time proving the young woman's innocence. It would take a miracle.

Terumi is seen in photos taken with a telephoto lens. She is in the car being driven from the prison to the court, wearing black sunglasses and a fringe that covers her entire forehead. She pulls up a white scarf to hide all or part of her face. However, by now, with the countless press articles published about her, the entire country of Japan knows the face of the murderer.

Throughout the hearings, Terumi continues to insist that she did not kill Sawako but merely dismembered and scattered parts of the body.

She explains that on that night, she left her apartment to go to the sharehouse. When she returned, she found her friend dead, lying face down near the front door, her face bloodied. Terumi did not immediately contact the police because she was afraid her loans would be discovered by the authorities. She also thought that it would be less painful for Sawako's family if she were simply missing, rather than dead (which is debatable).

January 1:
4:55 AM – How long before a body starts to smell?
4:58 AM – How to prevent a body from decomposing?
5:47 AM – Ten ways to dispose of a corpse if you really need to.
6:25 AM – How long does it take to inherit from someone who is missing?
6:34 AM – How to dispose of body parts?
9:29 AM – What does formaldehyde do[1]?
9:34 AM – How long does DNA evidence last?
9:59 AM – Can identification be done on partial remains?
11:34 AM – Dismemberment and the best ways to dispose of a body
11:44 AM – How to clean blood from a wooden floor?
11:56 AM – Luminol to detect blood.
1:08 PM – What happens when you put body parts in ammonia?
1:21 PM – Is it better to dispose of crime scene clothes or wash them?

January 2:
12:45 PM – Metal saw best tool for dismemberment.
1:10 PM – Can you be accused of murder without a body?
1:14 PM – Can a body be identified with broken teeth?

January 3:
1:02 PM – What happens to the hair on a corpse?
1:13 PM – What is the decomposition rate of a body found in a plastic bag compared to one found in the woods?

Brian Walshe has nevertheless chosen to plead not guilty and is, as I write these lines, awaiting his trial.

[1] In its liquid form, it is formaldehyde, used to preserve bodies.

This characteristic (or perhaps even psychiatric deviance) in the young woman, the desire to conceal the truth, supposedly to ease others' suffering, becomes apparent.

Terumi states: "I intended to bury the body in a nearby park or under some flowers near a school, and I would have gone to pray for her from time to time. . . But then I decided to cut it into several pieces. Unfortunately, the whole body didn't fit in my freezer, so I took part of it to the sharehouse."

The defense argued that Sawako could have been murdered by someone else during the fifteen minutes Terumi left her alone in the apartment. Regarding the credit card, she also claimed that Sawako had lent it to her and given her permission to withdraw the money.

Terumi's lawyers have only one card to play, in reality: the tragic childhood of the accused. Her abuse, her rapes, her stillborn child... Terrible episodes that undoubtedly impact the participants in the trial. The defense relies on this to seek a reduction in her sentence, hoping to prevent her from being sentenced to the death penalty, which is still in effect in Japan for violent crimes. Does she suffer from psychiatric problems? The medical professionals do not make a clear decision on this matter. However, there is a noted tendency for her to conceal things from everyone in order to spare others from spreading her own trauma. And so, she would have dismembered her victim to prevent her family from finding her dead. It's a light explanation, put that way. But the twists and turns of the human soul...

With all the evidence at her disposal, including the identity theft of the victim, her search history on the internet, and her communications on various networks, including WhatsApp, the prosecution was able to refute all these claims and successfully demonstrate Terumi's intent to murder Sawako and then make her disappear.

The verdict doesn't take long to arrive. Terumi Morishima, found guilty on all counts, is sentenced to life imprisonment by the professional judges of the Osaka District Court. Despite an immediate appeal from her defense team to the High Court of Japan, the verdict is upheld.

The same occurs after a final appeal to the Supreme Court in September 2018. Nothing changes. The life sentence is confirmed. In this final review, Judge Shibayama declares: “In order to hide the evidence of your murder, you completely destroyed the body. It can be said that this was a cruel act, with particularly malicious criminality, for which your responsibility is heavy.”

Terumi’s decision to kill Sawako was likely influenced by a combination of early trauma, childhood sexual abuse, and the high financial demands of living in a large Japanese metropolis.

Her lack of stable employment, the absence of family and friends, and the many hours she spent alone online at home may have led her to feel desperately isolated and to spiral into crime.

Terumi might not have felt the need to ruin someone else’s life if she had had more money and access to psychological care to help improve her life, both financially and emotionally.

But with ifs. . . If life were that simple and everything always went perfectly in the best of all possible worlds, should we then imagine that crime would disappear from the human world?

ROOM
or RENT
POLICE

"BOOKS TO SPAN THE EAST AND WEST"

Tuttle Publishing was founded in 1832 in the small New England town of Rutland, Vermont [USA]. Our core values remain as strong today as they were then—to publish best-in-class books which bring people together one page at a time. In 1948, we established a publishing outpost in Japan—and Tuttle is now a leader in publishing English-language books about the arts, languages and cultures of Asia. The world has become a much smaller place today and Asia's economic and cultural influence has grown. Yet the need for meaningful dialogue and information about this diverse region has never been greater. Over the past seven decades, Tuttle has published thousands of books on subjects ranging from martial arts and paper crafts to language learning and literature—and our talented authors, illustrators, designers and photographers have won many prestigious awards. We welcome you to explore the wealth of information available on Asia at **www.tuttlepublishing.com**.

Published by Tuttle Publishing, an imprint of Periplus Editions (HK) Ltd.

www.tuttlepublishing.com

ISBN: 978-4-8053-1999-4
Library of Congress Cataloging-in Publication Data is in process.

Distributed by

North America, Latin America & Europe
Tuttle Publishing
364 Innovation Drive
North Clarendon, VT
05759-9436, USA
Tel: 1 (802) 773 8930; Fax: 1 (802) 773 6993
info@tuttlepublishing.com; www.tuttlepublishing.com

Japan
Tuttle Publishing
Yaekari Building 3rd Floor
5-4-12 Osaki
Shinagawa-ku
Tokyo 141-0032
Tel: (81) 3 5437-0171; Fax: (81) 3 5437-0755
sales@tuttle.co.jp; www.tuttle.co.jp

Asia Pacific
Berkeley Books Pte. Ltd.
3 Kallang Sector #04-01
Singapore 349278
Tel: (65) 67412178; Fax: (65) 67412179
inquiries@periplus.com.sg; www.tuttlepublishing.com

GPSR representative
Matt Parsons
matt.parsons@upi2mbooks.hr
UPI-2M PLUS d.o.o., Medulićeva 20, 10000 Zagreb, Croatia

30 29 28 27 26 25 6 5 4 3 2 1
Printed in Malaysia 2507VP